KU-770-989

# CHILDREN'S
# CONCISE
# HISTORY
# ENCYCLOPEDIA

General Editor and Consultant: Brian Williams
House Editor: Brenda Apsley
Art Direction: Bob Swan
Design and Layout: Melissa Orrom-Swan
Typesetting: Andrew Maddock/Colourfield Limited
Index: Ian Horn

*Artists*
Mark Stacey
Alan Langford
Michael Codd
Phil Harding
Peter Bull
John James
James Field

Copyright © 1993 World International Publishing Limited.
Published in Great Britain by World International Publishing Limited,
An Egmont Company, Egmont House, PO Box 111,
Great Ducie Street, Manchester M60 3BL.

ISBN 0-7498-0843-8

Printed in Spain

World Horizons is an imprint of World International Publishing Limited.
All rights reserved. No part of this publication may be reproduced,
stored in a retrieval system, or transmitted, in any form or by any
means, electronic, mechanical, photocopying, recording, or otherwise,
without prior permission of the copyright owners.

*A catalogue record for this book is available from the British Library*

World
HORIZONS

# CHILDREN'S
# CONCISE
# HISTORY
# ENCYCLOPEDIA

## NEIL GRANT

# Contents

# Introduction

History is the story of the human race. Everybody, every little village, every event – never mind how unimportant – is part of history if there is any record of it. But history books tell only part of the story. This book is a guide to human history since the beginnings of human society down to the present, but it can record only the most important events and the most famous people. Perhaps it would be just as interesting to read about peaceful villagers whose way of life goes on in the same way for centuries. But history is also about change. It shows us how we came to be what we are, how we changed from being simple hunters living much like other animals to become creators of huge cities, spaceships and horribly powerful weapons – among other things. History books like this one therefore record only the great changes that have taken place in the world.

Great changes may happen quickly, or they may take many centuries. One thing should be obvious from an encyclopedia of world history: the speed of change is not always the same. In fact, it gets faster and faster as we approach modern times.

The increasing speed of change is not steady. There seem to be times when changes happen extra-fast. One of these times occurred in Europe during the Renaissance of the 16th century, another in the Industrial Revolution of the early 19th century. Since then the speed of change has gone on increasing. Will it ever slow down? And what will happen if it doesn't? Fortunately, those are questions which writers of history do not have to answer!

An encyclopedia is a reference book, a book for looking up facts. It is important to understand how it is arranged. This book is divided into chronological sections, from the earliest times to the present. Each section contains several chapters which are listed in the Contents (page 4). At the end of each section is a page of References, which gives short descriptions of people and things not explained in the text.

To find out about any subject, the first place to look is the Index at the back of the book. That will tell you every page on which the subject is mentioned, whether it is in the main text, the captions to the pictures, or the Reference pages.

# Ancient Times

# Hunters

When the last Ice Age ended, about 11,000 years ago, human beings had been living on Earth for thousands of years. They had already taken the first steps which separated them from all other animals. They still depended on the natural environment for all their needs, but they had begun the battle to conquer nature which was to make them the rulers of the Earth.

## Stone Age technology

People looked for food as animals do, gathering roots, leaves and berries. They hunted for meat, as well as skins to make clothes. Families had to move in search of new food supplies, and so they lived in temporary shelters or camps. Sometimes, when they found a lake full of fish, for example, they were able to settle down and form larger groups, or tribes.

People had the first essentials to make them less dependent on nature – shelter, clothing and tools. They made their tools and weapons from wood, bone, horn and stone. Flint was especially useful, because it could be shaped by flaking off thin slices to make a sharp cutting edge. Many Stone Age tools have been found and can be seen in museums today. They include the stone axes, with wooden handles, with which men began to clear the dense forest that then covered almost all of what is now Europe.

After trying to float on logs, people learned how to make canoes from hollowed-out tree trunks or from skins on a wooden frame. They caught fish with barbed harpoons, or with nets, and perhaps lines. Nets were also useful for trapping birds, but the main hunting weapons were bows and arrows.

Larger animals, like the mammoth or woolly rhinoceros, were caught in traps and speared to death. Hunters threw spears with the help of a spear-thrower, a notched stick which acted like an extra length of the thrower's arm. The wild dogs that followed the hunters for scraps were gradually tamed, and trained to help in the hunt.

*Stone Age men were the hunters and women stayed 'at home' with the children. Inset: A flint tool.*

### The spread of mankind

Our earliest ancestors lived in Africa, Asia and Europe, but not in the Americas or Australia. During the Ice Age, it was possible to walk from Siberia to Alaska across the frozen Bering Strait, and that was how the ancestors of the American Indians arrived, roughly 30,000 years ago. About 20,000 years ago the ancestors of the Aborigines reached Australia by a land bridge, crossing from south-east Asia via what are now the islands of Indonesia without getting their feet wet.

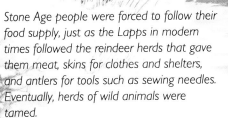

*Stone Age people were forced to follow their food supply, just as the Lapps in modern times followed the reindeer herds that gave them meat, skins for clothes and shelters, and antlers for tools such as sewing needles. Eventually, herds of wild animals were tamed.*

### THE SPEED OF CHANGE

Although many important changes took place in prehistoric times, the speed at which they happened was very slow compared with the speed of change in modern times. The time that has passed since civilization began, soon after the end of the last Ice Age, is less than one-tenth of the time the human race has existed. After the Ice Age, the speed of change began to increase, and it has been increasing at an ever greater rate since.

### STONE AGE ART

Although we have a good idea of how Stone Age people lived, we do not know what they thought or felt. The most amazing examples of their culture were only discovered in the last century. They are the animal paintings made on the walls of caves in southern France and northern Spain. Deep in the ground, they must have been made by torchlight, and they probably had some 'magic' purpose, perhaps to bring success in hunting. The earliest ones were made about 20,000 BC and the latest about 9000 BC. The painters seem to have known most of the basic methods used in the arts today.

# Farmers

The biggest change in the story of the human race happened before written records began. It was not a sudden change. In fact it was spread over thousands of years. It was a change in the way people obtained food. Instead of depending entirely on what they could catch or find in the wild, they began to grow their own. They became farmers. This was the first step on the road to what we call 'civilization'.

The hunters of the Old Stone Age had dogs, and some tribes may have tamed other animals. Some experts believe that horses were domesticated 1,000 years or more before farming began, and cattle may have been kept in East Africa even earlier. However, it was not until about 8000 BC that people grew crops.

## The Fertile Crescent

The first farmers lived in a band of country which ran from the Persian Gulf, through the valleys of the Tigris and Euphrates rivers to the Turkish border, then turned towards the eastern shore of the Mediterranean and the Red Sea. The Fertile Crescent, which was much wetter then than it is now, is still dotted with the remains of some of the world's oldest cities.

Among the food gathered in this region were wild cereal grasses. A family could collect enough grain from these to last all year, so they did not have to go wandering in search of new food supplies. At some time people must have noticed that certain types of cereal grass produced bigger seeds, or grain, and they began to sow that type themselves. This idea slowly spread to other settlements, through trade and the movements of people.

Crop growing began in China and south-east Asia about the same time, or perhaps some centuries later. There, the cereal was a different crop, an early form of millet. Rice, which was to be the most useful cereal in that part of the world, came later. In Mexico and Central America, crop growing began about 5000 BC, and the main crop was maize, or sweetcorn.

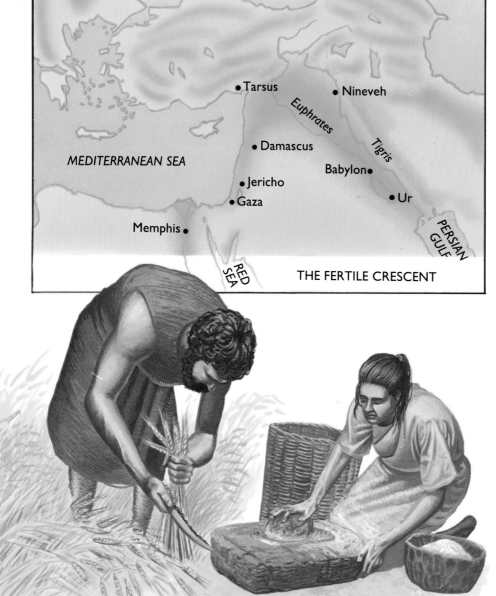

THE FERTILE CRESCENT

*At harvest time, people cut wild wheat with a flint sickle on a horn handle. They grasped a bunch of stalks with one hand and cut with the other, using a sawing movement. Women pounded the grain into flour and baked flat loaves of bread on hot stones or in simple ovens.*

Goats, sheep and pigs were kept for milk, wool and meat.

## METALS

People first began to use copper in about 7000 BC. Though easy to separate from the ore, and easy to hammer into shape, copper is very soft. People soon learned how to mix it with tin to form an alloy called bronze, a harder and more useful metal. This early, metal-using period is therefore called the Bronze Age.

Iron is a more useful metal still (the Aztecs of Mexico valued it more than gold), but people were unable to make iron until after about 2000 BC.

These changes in technology happened at widely different times in different places. For example, the Chinese were making cast iron 1,500 years before the Europeans; the Americans never did invent the wheel.

### Farm animals

Herds of wild sheep and goats roamed the grasslands of the Fertile Crescent; people had probably learned to control them before they learned how to plant crops. Pigs and cattle were domesticated later and, in this region, so were horses, which were to have a great effect on human history through their use in war. The wild horses ridden by Scythian nomads were quite small – too small to carry a rider over long distances. Probably the early horse owners learned how to breed and develop certain types of animals, such as the war or plough horse.

The plough was first used in Mesopotamia in about 3500 BC and spread to Europe much later. The first ploughs were little more than pointed sticks which scratched up the surface. The soil could not be turned until iron became available to give the plough a hard cutting edge.

# Cities and Craftsmen

To this day, a few people in remote places still live by hunting and gathering, but it was farming that led to the main line of development in human society. Farming made town life possible. We often speak of 'town' and 'country' as if they were opposites, but the town depends on the country for food. By making the country produce more food – by farming – towns could grow.

## Farming

A family which lives by hunting and gathering needs thousands of acres to provide enough wild food. But a family which lives by farming needs only 10 to 20 acres. One result of farming was that the population began to grow, and many more people could live in a small area.

Farming people produced more food than they needed to feed themselves. What was left over could be traded for other goods. For city life, trade is almost as important as farming.

Farming also allowed people – or rather, some people – more leisure time. The workers in the fields probably worked harder than their hunting ancestors, but society was becoming divided into different classes of people. In a hunting society, everyone was more or less equal, because everyone was busy doing the same job – collecting food. Once food production became a specialized job, other people could spend their lives as craftsmen, traders, priests, magistrates and so on.

Different jobs had different ranks. Priests, for example, had a higher status than farm workers or craftsmen.

Above: *City life produced many new professions. Scribes kept written records of trade, production and taxes. Bards provided entertainment, telling stories accompanied by music. Traders exchanged goods with other cities, sometimes far away.*

Below: *Some cities were built before people discovered how to grow crops. The ancient city of Jericho, which had stone walls and a tower before 6000 BC, was a trade centre. Its citizens could gather enough wild wheat to provide food throughout the year.*

## Civilization

Farming, and the changes which followed, created the conditions in which civilization could develop. But what is 'civilization'? It is not easy to say. It is connected with city life and large buildings, with a written language, perhaps with law and religion and the arts; but none of those things tell us what civilization is, and there were many different forms of civilization in ancient times. Compared with earlier times, civilization was much more complicated, and changes happened much more easily. Among hunters and gatherers, who lead a nomadic life, life does not change. Civilization, with all its complications, cannot develop among people who are on the move.

## War

Some people would say that another characteristic of civilization is warfare. So far as we know, war did not exist among our hunting/gathering ancestors. However, that may be because they lived in small groups, thinly scattered over a large region. They certainly had fights.

When cities appeared, they were usually built with strong walls. Obviously the people were afraid of being attacked. By whom? Rival cities, perhaps, but also by other peoples who had not developed city life. For thousands of years, cities were to be tempting targets for bands of marauding nomads.

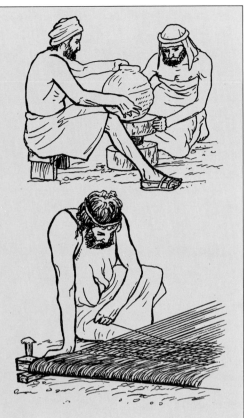

### POTTERS AND WEAVERS

Pottery – making vessels of clay baked hard in an oven – is one of the oldest crafts. The first clay vessels in the Middle East were made before 6000 BC. It was a great advance. People could drink soup or beer more easily, and food could be stored more safely.

The earliest cups and bowls were moulded by hand from a lump of clay, but by 3000 BC potters in the Middle East were 'throwing' pots on a wheel, which was turned by an assistant while the potter shaped the clay.

Pottery may break, but the pieces are not easily destroyed, and pottery sherds are one of the most important types of archaeological evidence from ancient times. Cloth, on the other hand, quickly rots, but we know that the craft of weaving wool into cloth was known in the Middle East at roughly the same time as the first pottery was made.

*The war between raiding nomads and settled townspeople continued in parts of Asia and Africa into modern times.*

# Mesopotamia

Civilization began in certain large river valleys in the Near East and Asia roughly 5,000 years ago. The earliest civilizations probably developed separately, although there was soon some contact between them. In the Americas, civilization began much later, but the Americans knew nothing of other civilizations until modern times.

### The Sumerians

Civilization was born in Mesopotamia (modern Iraq), the 'land between two rivers' (Tigris and Euphrates). The Sumerians settled in the hot, flat, swampy south before 4000 BC, building dykes and canals to water their fields and to protect their villages from floods. They had a complicated and powerful religion and, from about 3500 BC, their cities grew up around religious shrines. At Ur, the most famous of them, the inner city was a kind of sacred precinct where people came to seek justice or pay taxes to the priests, who were agents of the god who 'owned' the city.

The Sumerians were not a 'nation'. The cities were independent, with their own kings (who were also high priests), and they often made war on each other. They were built mainly of bricks made from river mud baked hard in the sun. A few big temples or palaces were built of stone, but building stone, like wood, had to be imported.

The Sumerians invented the first written language, writing on clay tablets with a pointed reed. Some tablets have been found, and so have works of art in gold and precious stones, sculptures, musical instruments, toys and board games made of ivory. The Sumerians were interested in mathematics. Their basic unit was 60. That is why we have 60 minutes in an hour and 360 (6 x 60) degrees in a circle.

Right: *A helmet from Ur.*
Below right: *Some Sumerian temples and palaces were as big as cathedrals. Bigger still was the ziggurat of Ur, a kind of artificial mountain on top of which (the Sumerians believed) lived the chief god, watching over the citizens.*

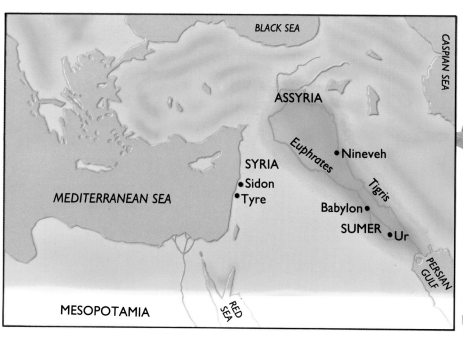

Above: *The 'Standard of Ur', made of coloured stones and shells, shows scenes of war and peace. This section shows warriors, prisoners and charioteers.*

## Babylon and Assyria

Sumerian civilization lasted over 1,000 years. In fact, although the Sumerians themselves disappeared, their civilization lived on, in changing forms, in the later empires of the Middle East.

The greatest of these empires were Babylon and Assyria, which existed side by side, sometimes at peace, sometimes at war, from the 19th to the 7th century BC. The Babylonians in particular made many new contributions to the growth of civilization, such as King Hammurabi's Code of Laws and the first astronomical instrument, the astrolabe.

The main contribution of the Assyrians was to the art of war. With little fertile land of their own, these warlike, bearded people, with their speedy, knife-wheeled chariots, set out to conquer their neighbours. At the height of their power, in about 700 BC, their empire stretched from Egypt to the Persian (or Arabian) Gulf. They destroyed Babylon, but in 627 BC a new Babylonian empire arose. The great desert city was restored on a grand scale. The Hanging Gardens of Babylon were long remembered as one of the Seven Wonders of the World.

In the 6th century BC the last of the ancient empires of the Middle East arose – the empire of the Persians, led by Cyrus the Great. They conquered New Babylon in 539 BC and built up the greatest empire yet, stretching from Egypt to India.

### GILGAMESH

The Epic of Gilgamesh tells of the adventures of a Sumerian hero who was probably based on a real person, a king of the city of Uruk who lived before 2500 BC. The earliest copy of the text was found on clay tablets in the royal library of the Assyrian king, Ashurbanipal. He lived in the 7th century BC, but some of the tablets are centuries older.

The Gilgamesh epic contains some stories like those in the Bible (which was written later), including a story of a Great Flood.

# Ancient Egypt

The Ancient Egyptians created the first national state, which was founded when a king called Menes united Upper and Lower Egypt in about 3100 BC. Among other achievements, the Ancient Egyptians raised the largest buildings in the world. But the most remarkable fact about Egyptian civilization was that it lasted so long – nearly 3,000 years. It was fully formed by about 2600 BC, and although changes happened, it was still much the same kind of civilization when Alexander the Great conquered it in 332 BC.

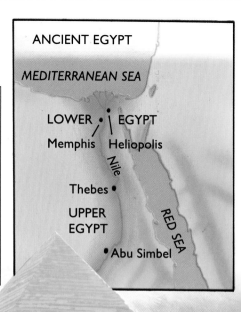

ANCIENT EGYPT

MEDITERRANEAN SEA

LOWER • ᵢ EGYPT
Memphis  Heliopolis
Nile
Thebes •
UPPER
EGYPT
RED SEA
• Abu Simbel

**Egypt and the River Nile**

Egypt was well defended by nature. It was surrounded by desert, sea and, in the south, swamps. In the end foreign conquerors did overcome it, but for many centuries it was free from serious attack.

Egypt depended entirely on the River Nile. In a way, the Nile *was* Egypt, providing water and the main highway, and rich farming land. Every year it flooded, covering the valley with a layer of rich, damp silt in which the Egyptians sowed their crops.

## THE PYRAMIDS

The chief pyramids were built about 4,500 years ago by huge gangs of workers. At that time the Egyptians did not have wheeled carts or pulleys. The stone blocks, weighing two or three tonnes, were moved on large barges and then on rollers and up ramps into position. The stone had to be cut with copper chisels, as iron smelting had not been invented. These buildings were huge. The Great Pyramid of Khufu was 147m (480ft) high. It can still be seen at Giza, near Cairo, though it is a little shorter now.

## Pharaoh and people

The ruler of Egypt was called the pharaoh. He was not only a king, but a god, and was worshipped along with many other gods, such as the Sun god Ra, the falcon-headed god Horus and the ibis-headed god of wisdom, Thoth. Below the pharaoh came nobles and priests, then scribes or clerks, who kept detailed records of government business, and finally the farmers, craftsmen and workers, many of whom were slaves. Egyptian schoolboys were urged to work hard so that they might become scribes.

On the irrigated fields, people grew cereal crops, vegetables, grapes for wine and flax for making linen. They kept sheep, goats, pigs, cattle, ducks and geese – but not chickens. The Egyptians traded with other peoples around the Mediterranean, and even sent ships down the Red Sea to East Africa to buy frankincense and other rare products.

Taxes were high, and besides having to give a large part of their crops to the government, ordinary people had to work on building the temples and palaces of the pharaohs. Although they were poor and overworked, Egypt was a rich land and there were many religious holidays.

Right: *Rich Egyptians hunted wildfowl from punts in the Nile delta, helped by tame cats and sometimes accompanied by their families.*

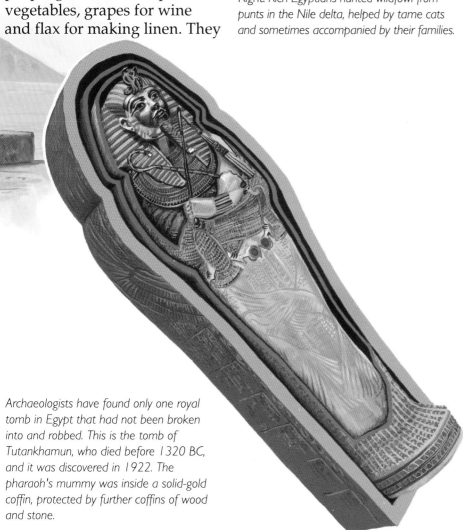

*Archaeologists have found only one royal tomb in Egypt that had not been broken into and robbed. This is the tomb of Tutankhamun, who died before 1320 BC, and it was discovered in 1922. The pharaoh's mummy was inside a solid-gold coffin, protected by further coffins of wood and stone.*

## Tombs and mummies

The Egyptians believed in life after death. They thought people had to take with them everything they would need in the next world – including their bodies. Bodies of important people were preserved by mummification – taking out the insides (the brain was pulled out through the nose), soaking the bodies in soda, then drying and wrapping them in bandages. Buried in several coffins in stone tombs, bodies could be preserved for centuries.

Tombs were painted with scenes from the dead person's life, showing family, servants and possessions. Such paintings, together with sculptures also found in tombs, tell us much of what we know about life in Ancient Egypt.

# Crete and Mycenae

The civilization which developed on the Mediterranean island of Crete before 2000 BC is especially interesting. It was the distant forerunner of Classical Greece, and it may therefore be said to mark the beginning of Western civilization. It was only rediscovered in this century, and was called 'Minoan' after King Minos, a king of Crete who is a figure in Greek legend.

## The Minoans

The capital of Minoan Crete was Knossos, which was probably the biggest city built up to that time. It may have held over 100,000 people. It was a wealthy place, and its wealth came from the sea. The Minoans were a seagoing people, who traded with Egypt, Greece, Spain and other areas and controlled the shipping routes of the Mediterranean. Sea power protected Crete from foreign attack: Knossos had no city walls.

We know very little about life in Minoan Crete. Some mysteries would be solved if we understood its languages. The first written language was a form of picture writing. By 1500 BC two languages with signs to represent syllables were in use. One of them we do not understand at all. The other seems to have been an early form of Greek.

Minoan art and religion may also have influenced Greece, although the chief Minoan deity was a goddess. She was often represented, in beautifully made statuettes, holding snakes, symbols of good health. Splendid, realistic paintings have been found on the palace walls.

Above left: *The magnificent palace at Knossos was five storeys high and as big as two football pitches. Besides royal chambers, it contained workshops, storerooms and living quarters for other people.*

Left: *The bull was a very important animal to the Minoans, perhaps worshipped for its strength. The strange practice of 'bull-vaulting' appears in paintings. It was probably some kind of religious ceremony, not a sporting event.*

## Mycenae

Minoan civilization disappeared about 1400 BC. Earthquake and fire may have been to blame, or its fall may have been due to conquest by the Mycenaeans. They were a Greek-speaking people from mainland Greece, and they became the successors of the Minoans. They took over the Minoans' trade and colonies, as well as many of their customs, and in time became equally wealthy.

Unlike the Minoans, the Mycenaeans lived in independent city-states, although they sometimes acted together under the leadership of the greatest, Mycenae. We know that they had a trading post at the city of Troy. The famous story of the siege of Troy told by the Greek poet Homer may have been based on real events. But the cause of the war was more likely a quarrel over trade than the kidnap of the queen, Helen.

The siege of Troy probably took place before 1200 BC. By that time things were changing as a new race of people, the Dorians, were invading Greece from the north. Like the Minoans before them, the Mycenaeans disappeared from history.

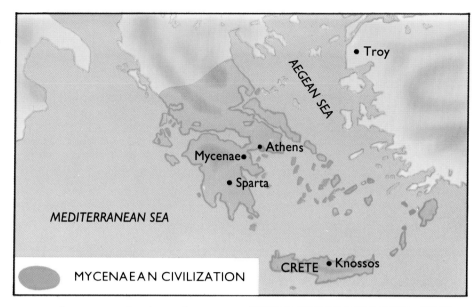

MYCENAEAN CIVILIZATION

*The towns and royal tombs of the Mycenaeans, containing fabulous gold ornaments, were discovered by the German archaeologist Heinrich Schliemann in the 1870s, not long before Sir Arthur Evans discovered Knossos.*

### THE PHOENICIANS

The people known as the Phoenicians settled on the eastern coast of the Mediterranean before 2000 BC. After the fall of the Mycenaeans, in about 1200 BC, the Phoenicians became the chief sea power. In their tough little ships they sailed as far as West Africa and Cornwall, where they traded for tin. They controlled the best source of timber in the region (the cedars of Lebanon), they produced glass, carved ivory and an expensive purple dye made from shellfish. On land they were not powerful. Their homeland was conquered by the Assyrians in the 7th century BC, although the Phoenician colony of Carthage survived to become a great power.

The Phoenicians made one huge advance in civilization. They invented an alphabet, in which the symbols (or letters) represented sounds. This is the basis of our alphabet today.

# China and India

Civilization and large cities appeared in eastern Asia later than the Middle East but, so far as we know, quite independently. The first civilization of southern Asia began a little earlier. It too probably arose independently, although it was in touch with the Middle East at an early stage.

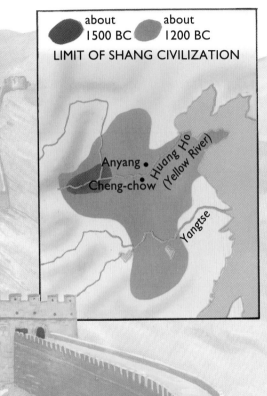

about 1500 BC   about 1200 BC

LIMIT OF SHANG CIVILIZATION

Anyang
Cheng-chow
Huang Ho (Yellow River)
Yangtse

The Great Wall of China was begun by a Chin emperor. It was said that one in three Chinese men worked on the construction.

## Han China

The earliest centre of Chinese civilization was the Huang Ho, or Yellow River, where farming villages had existed since about 5000 BC. A Bronze Age society developed here before 1500 BC, and produced works of art which we can recognize as Chinese in style. A simple form of picture writing existed, and so did money, in the form of shells and bones, and perhaps chopsticks. The Chinese learned how to make silk, and by 500 BC they were using iron tools.

Society was still tribal, led by warrior lords with large estates, and the area of civilization was small (about the size of England). Gradually it spread, especially to the fertile south. By the time China was united under the Han dynasty (206 BC to AD 220), the general pattern of civilization was already formed, and was not to be broken until the revolutions of the 20th century.

The Chinese were divided into a small class of landowners and a large mass of poor peasants. The upper class claimed descent from gods or heroes. The king ('the Son of Heaven') was more of a god than a ruler, with little power over the great landlords. But besides their gods and religious beliefs, and their fondness for consulting oracles, the Chinese were always a practical people. The great Chinese prophets preached a very worldly kind of religion. They were more interested in life on Earth than life after death.

CHINESE DYNASTIES

Chinese history is divided into dynasties, or ruling families. They tend to form a pattern. A new dynasty, fresh and lively, brings peace, prosperity and strong government. But after some time it weakens, government breaks down, and fortunes decline until a new dynasty takes over. Early dynasties are known through legend. The first known from historical evidence is the Shang.

| | |
|---|---|
| Shang | about 1500–1027 BC |
| Chou | 1027–771 BC (Western lands lost) |
| Eastern Chou | 771–221 BC ('Warring States' period from 475) |
| Chin | 221–206 BC (this dynasty gave China its name) |
| Han | 206 BC–AD 220 (split into two from AD 25) |

## The Indus valley

The great valley of the River Indus, in modern Pakistan, provided the fertile soil in which the first Indian civilization took root. It covered a wide area – the largest cities, Mohenjo Daro and Harappa, were nearly 1,600 kilometres (1,000 miles) apart – and it lasted roughly a thousand years. When it was overrun by invaders from the north-west in about 1500 BC, its gods, works of art, even styles in clothes and jewellery, were definitely 'Indian'.

The Indus cities were built of brick. They had wide streets built on a grid pattern, huge temples, monuments and public baths, warehouses covering about 3,000 square metres (about 3,500 square yards) and better drains and sewers than many places have today. Farming was very profitable in the rich soil.

*The chaos and war of the later Chou period caused much debate about government and morality. The greatest figure of the time was the teacher Confucius (K'ung Fu-tzu),above, who was born about 550 BC. In later times his teaching became a kind of religion, but what he really taught was a way of life – good behaviour and respect for tradition.*

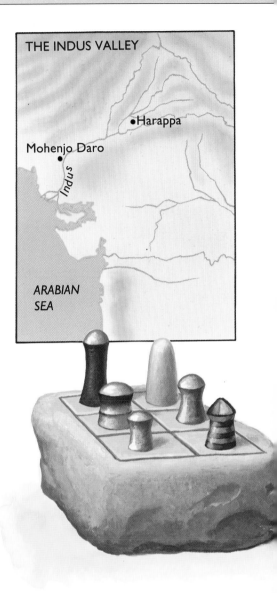

THE INDUS VALLEY

Harappa

Mohenjo Daro

Indus

ARABIAN SEA

*The Indus valley people played a game something like chess and made clay toys .*

The climate was different then, and places that are very dry today may have had heavy rain. The Indus valley was probably the place where cotton was first grown. Surplus food was exported in exchange for materials such as copper. We know little about how people lived, for archaeologists did not excavate in the Indus valley until the 1920s, and no one yet has been able to understand the Indus picture writing.

# *References*

**Aborigines** The original inhabitants of Australia, whose customs can help us understand how Stone Age people lived.

**Akkadians** A people who lived in the Euphrates valley and, under Sargon I, conquered Mesopotamia, creating an empire that lasted from about 2370 to 2160 BC.

**Alexander the Great** (356–323 BC) King of Macedon, who conquered Greece and the Persian empire, including Egypt.

**Altamira** The site of caves in Spain which, with Lascaux in France, contains the finest paintings, mainly of animals, of the Old Stone Age.

**Archaeology** The study of human life in the past through relics such as the contents of graves, buried towns, ruins, etc.

**Cro-Magnon** The name given to an early race of human beings, from the Cro-Magnon cave in France.

**Cuneiform** Writing with wedge-shaped symbols, developed by the Sumerians from picture-writing.

**Delta** The swampy, D-shaped area of land at the mouth of the Nile (and some other rivers), where the main river divides into channels.

**Dorians** A people who began to invade Greece in large numbers in about 1200 BC, ending the Mycenaean civilization.

**Dynasty** A ruling house or family, or a line of kings.

**Epic** A story, especially in poetry, of heroes and great deeds.

**Fire** Used by our ancestors about 400,000 years ago, when they 'captured' some from a natural, forest fire; they learned that wooden points could be hardened in flames, and that animals feared fire; but it was a long time before they learned to make fire themselves, by friction.

**Flint** A very hard stone which can be chipped away in flakes to make cutting and chopping tools; in later times it was used to make fire by striking flint against steel.

**Frankincense** A sweet-smelling gum, obtained from certain East African and Arabian trees and used for perfume and incense; the ancient Egyptians used a lot of it in religious ceremonies.

**Hammurabi** King of Babylon, which reached the height of its power in his reign, about 1792–1750 BC; a law-giver, he established the legal principle of an eye for an eye.

**Hierarchy** The system of rank or order of people belonging to an institution, such as a church, with each rank inferior to the one above.

**Hittites** A people who conquered an empire in eastern Turkey and Syria and, thanks to their advanced iron weapons, dominated most of the Middle East from about 1500 to 1200 BC.

**Homo sapiens** ('thinking' or 'wise man') The species of mammal to which human beings belong; earlier varieties of human included *Homo erectus* ('upright man') and *Homo habilis* ('tool-using man').

**Ice Age** A very cold period, when sheets of ice covered large parts of the world; in the last Ice Age, which ended about 11,000 years ago, much of Europe and North America was covered.

**Lao Tzu** (about 604–531 BC) Chinese philosopher, the founder of Taoism; he preached sympathy with nature and aloofness from worldly ambitions.

**Lapps** or **Sami** People of northern Scandinavia, who led a nomadic life following the reindeer herds, even into the present century.

**Lascaux** *See* **Altamira.**

**Mesopotamia** The land of the two rivers (Tigris and Euphrates), roughly the area of modern Iraq, where civilization first began.

**Migration** The movement of peoples, or nations, from one region to another; in early times, people were often forced to migrate to seek new food supplies, or land.

**Nineveh** The Assyrian capital, a magnificent city excavated by a British archaeologist in the 19th century; relief sculptures showing Assyrian triumphs, and thousands of clay tablets from the royal library, are now in the British Museum, London.

**Nomads** People who live on the move, making temporary homes where necessary; some nomads live by hunting and gathering, some keep animals, and some stay long enough in one place to plant and reap a harvest.

**Oracles** Prophets who used signs or help from the gods to foretell the future; the early Chinese sometimes cracked a human skull and interpreted the pattern of cracks.

**Picture writing** The earliest form of writing, in which simple pictures or symbols stood for objects like a man, the sun, water, etc.

**Prehistory** The story of the human race before written records.

**Relief sculpture** Carving in which, unlike 'free-standing' sculpture, the figures remain attached to the stone background.

**Scythians** A people from central Asia, skilled archers and horsemen, who moved south in about 700 BC and formed an empire in the Middle East.

**Seals** Carved surfaces, usually shaped like a cylinder, which left an impression when rolled over a clay tablet; many seals (or their impressions) have survived, providing important archaeological evidence.

**Sherds** or **shards** Fragments of pottery.

**Stone Age** The earliest age of human existence, when people used stone tools. Beginning 50,000 or so years ago and ending with the Bronze Age (about 2500 BC in Mesopotamia), it is divided into the Old Stone Age, or Palaeolithic era; Middle Stone Age, or Mesolithic; and New Stone Age, or Neolithic.

# *The Classical Age*

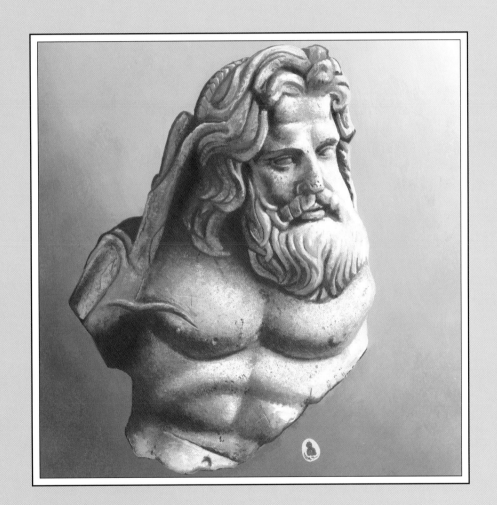

# The Greeks

The Classical civilization of Greece and Rome lasted over a thousand years, from its beginning in Greece in about 800 BC to the fall of Rome in AD 410. It is the foundation of modern, Western civilization. Our language, ideas and form of government can mostly be traced back to the Greeks.

## Freedom

The Greeks were not one nation. They were divided into what we call city-states, all of which were more or less independent. But they shared a language, customs and religion and, although they often fought each other, they regarded themselves as one people. They called all foreigners 'barbarians'. But what was the difference? The Greeks might have said: 'We are free men, but the barbarians are slaves'. Unlike earlier civilizations, which were ruled by all-powerful kings, the Greeks ruled themselves. In Athens, the greatest of the Greek city-states, every citizen could vote and might be appointed a government official. Not everyone was a citizen, however: you had to be male, and Athenian-born. Women lived a more restricted life.

The Greeks could think and say what they liked, without fear of punishment. Greek civilization was able to change and develop. The speed of change was much faster than in any other society before Western Europe during the Renaissance of the 16th century.

*The Greeks built temples as homes for their many gods and goddesses. The remains of some can still be seen.*

*Theatre developed in Greece out of religious ceremonies honouring the many gods and goddesses. Actors wore masks, a chorus provided singing and dancing, and spectators sat in the open, looking down on the 'orchestra'. Plays by Aeschylus, Euripides and Sophocles are still performed today.*

## Art and learning

Another important difference between Greek civilization and the earlier civilizations of the East is that we know far more about it. Some Classical Greek buildings, such as those on the Acropolis of Athens, are still standing, and Greek sculpture and pottery can be seen in any museum. More important than archaeological evidence, however, are the writings of the Greeks themselves.

Although much has been lost, we possess a large mass of Greek literature, including the first real works of history. Thanks to the historian Thucydides we know almost as much about the Peloponnesian War as we do about the Second World War.

Besides many forms of literature, the Greeks founded most forms of science and philosophy. Aristotle was the chief authority on biology, physics and other subjects for two thousand years after his death (322 BC). No real advance on Greek geometry and arithmetic was made until the 17th century. Philosophers today are still arguing about the ideas of Plato.

One thing is obvious: the Greeks were just as clever as we are! The difference between them and us is that we have over two thousand years of advancing knowledge to help us, while the Greeks started almost from nothing.

*The Greeks believed in physical fitness, and athletes travelled all over the country to take part in athletic contests. Even wars stopped during important festivals like the Olympic Games. According to legend, the first Olympic Games were held as early as 776 BC. Athletes were sometimes pictured on pottery (above) and in statues.*

*Athens was a great naval power, and the finest Greek warship was the trireme. It had three banks of oars and attacked by smashing into the oars of the enemy.*

### SLAVERY

All ancient societies had slaves, and the Greeks, in spite of their love of personal freedom, were no exception. Household slaves were usually well treated, but it was a different matter for those (mainly prisoners of war) who worked in the mines, like the silver mines in the territory of Athens. Men sent to work there often remained, working in narrow tunnels, until they died.

# Alexander the Great

After the Peloponnesian War, the struggle for power inside Greece continued. First Sparta reigned supreme, then Thebes took the lead; even Athens regained some of its naval strength. But by about 350 BC, all these powers had declined. A new power, Macedonia, moved in from the north. The Macedonians spoke Greek and had copied many Greek habits. Though the Greeks themselves did not regard them as fellow-Greeks, they were not quite barbarians either. Under an able king, Philip II, all of Greece was sucked into the Macedonian empire. When Athens was defeated in 338 BC, the age of the city-state came to an end.

*Alexander the Great lived from 356 to 323 BC. He was a supremely intelligent military strategist.*

## Alexander's conquests

Philip was succeeded by his son in 336 BC. Alexander had even bigger ambitions than his father. He launched an attack on the Persian empire, which had once ruled the eastern Greek cities and had been narrowly defeated by the mainland Greeks in the Persian Wars.

Alexander had amazing abilities. He was very intelligent (Aristotle had been his tutor) and he had a superhuman amount of energy. All his intelligence and energy was directed at military conquest – with astonishing results. At the head of a Greek and Macedonian army, he defeated and destroyed the huge Persian empire. But he did not stop there. For ten years his unbeatable army swept through the Middle East and into north-west India. In a famous battle near the River Jhelum (now in Pakistan) he defeated the Rajah Porus, whose army contained 200 trained elephants. He would have gone farther, but his men,

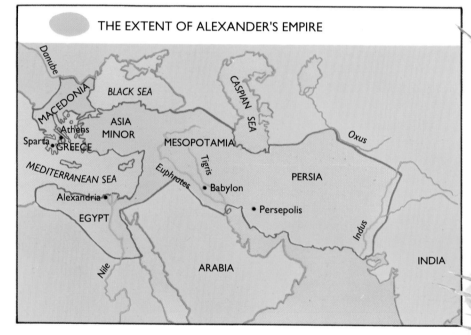

THE EXTENT OF ALEXANDER'S EMPIRE

who had followed him loyally for eight years, persuaded him to return. By the time of his death in 323 BC, when he was 32 years old, Alexander's empire covered almost all the ancient civilized world.

*Right: Against the powerful Persian cavalry, the Greeks fought in a solid block called a phalanx, which the cavalry could not break. Alexander also used cavalry and 'war machines' that could hurl a missile hundreds of metres.*

## THE PERSIAN EMPIRE

The Persian empire was created when Cyrus the Great rebelled against Babylonian rule in 550 BC. It became the largest empire ever known at that time, well-organized into 20 provinces, or *satrapies*, with elaborate laws, regular currency, good roads and an efficient postal service. The remains of the vast royal palace at Persepolis can still be seen, as can some traces of the first 'Suez Canal', between the Nile and the Red Sea, built by Darius I in about 520 BC. The Persian effort to conquer Greece was finally defeated in 480 BC, and in 334 BC Alexander the Great turned the tables by invading, and conquering, the Persian empire.

*Eratosthenes (276–194 BC) calculated the circumference of the Earth by measuring the angle of the Sun at Alexandria at noon on the day of the summer solstice. He knew that at Aswan the Sun at noon shone directly on to the bottom of a well, and was therefore directly overhead. He also knew the exact distance between Alexandria and Aswan. He found that the difference in the angle of the Sun was $\frac{1}{56}$ of a circle. Multiplying the distance by 56, Eratosthenes calculated the circumference of the Earth.*

**Hellenistic civilization**

Alexander's empire was a one-man affair. After his death it split up as his generals struggled for power. A more important effect of Alexander's conquests was the spread of Hellenistic ('Greek') civilization.

Throughout his empire, Alexander founded new towns (mostly named after himself). These towns were built in the Greek style, with Greek temples, Greek houses and Greek government. The city of Alexandria in Egypt became a centre of learning to rival Athens, where Eratosthenes first measured the size of the Earth, Archimedes worked out the principle of the screw, and Ptolemy wrote his great works on geography and astronomy.

The civilization that had begun in one small country became the civilization of the world. Greece itself was no longer a great country, but its spirit was inherited by a new and mightier European power, the empire of Rome.

# The Roman Republic

In the 7th century BC a few peasant-farmers lived in a group of villages on the River Tiber in central Italy. From these villages grew the greatest empire the world has ever seen. For a thousand years after it had ceased to exist, Roman civilization was the ideal which Europeans hoped to equal. Roman ideas and institutions inspired Europe well into modern times, and still have their influence today.

## The rise of Rome

In 509 BC the Romans rebelled against the Etruscan king who ruled them and set up an independent republic. The chief power was given to two consuls, who were elected by the people, and the Senate, a group of important citizens. Although it was a democratic system, in practice the upper class gained the upper hand.

Eventually, the struggle between the powerful few and the ordinary people was to bring the Republic to an end.

In its early years, the Republic was almost constantly at war with its neighbours. Though sometimes defeated, the Romans survived – and went on to conquer. By the 3rd century BC they were the most powerful people in Italy.

Above: *The Carthaginian general, Hannibal, defeated the Romans on the banks of the Trebia River (218 BC), his first major victory in Italy after his amazing march over the Alps. Though he often beat the Romans in battle, he could not conquer Rome.*

Rome's only rival in the western Mediterranean region was Carthage, in North Africa, which held land in Italy itself. War between the rivals was inevitable. In the First Punic (or Carthaginian) War, Rome gained Sicily. In the Second Punic War, the Romans were defeated many times by a great Carthaginian general called Hannibal (247–183 BC), who took his army, including elephants, across the Alps to invade Italy from the north. But in the end, Hannibal was forced to leave Italy and the Carthaginians were defeated. Later, their city was destroyed. Rome was left the greatest power in the region.

*The often-rebellious Roman people were kept happy with violent spectator sports. Gladiators fought to the death and criminals (including Christians who refused to worship Roman gods) were killed by wild animals.*

## THE RISE OF ROME

| | |
|---|---|
| 509 BC | The Romans expel their Etruscan rulers |
| 290 | Rome controls most of Italy |
| 264–241 | First Punic War |
| 218–201 | Second Punic War |
| 146 | Rome controls Greece |
| 149–146 | Third Punic War |
| 49 | Caesar conquers Gaul |
| 45 | Caesar becomes Rome's ruler |
| AD 27 | Octavian becomes the Emperor Augustus |

Below: *Upper-class Romans spent much of their leisure time at the public baths. The baths were like social clubs, where men could have a wrestling match or a chat over food and drink.*

## The fall of the republic

In the 2nd century, Rome was torn by civil war. The army became a force in government (as happens in unstable states today), and successful generals were able to seize power for themselves. The greatest of these generals was Julius Caesar (100–44 BC), who had conquered Gaul (roughly modern France) and even invaded the backward island of Britain. Having defeated his rival, Pompey, Caesar became the real ruler of Rome.

People feared he would make himself an emperor, like those all-powerful emperors of Egypt and the Middle East whom the republican Romans disliked as much as the Greeks did.

Caesar was a wise ruler, who at least restored law and order. He also introduced a new calendar – the one we use today. Whether he would have made himself emperor we shall never know, for he was soon murdered, and civil war broke out again. The winner was Caesar's adopted son, Octavian. Once he had made his position safe, Octavian did make himself emperor, taking a new name, Augustus. He kept all the officials and institutions of the republic, but they counted for little. The Emperor's word was law.

Left: *The Romans produced few thinkers to compare with the Greek philosophers. Their skills were more practical; they were expert builders and engineers. Some of their roads and buildings have lasted to the present day. Unlike the Greeks, they could make good concrete. This enabled them to build domes and arches, whereas the Greeks had built in straight lines, with beams and columns.*

# The People of Israel

Among the Semitic peoples of the ancient Middle East were the Israelites, later known as Hebrews (after their language), or Jews. They were a small nation, with no great armies, and for most of their history they were ruled by others. What made them important was their religion. Unlike other early religions, which had all kinds of gods and supernatural beings, the religion of the Israelites had one, all-powerful god. He was a god for the Israelites only, but the force of this idea of a single, supreme god was to shape the two most powerful world religions, Christianity and Islam.

## The kingdom of David

The Hebrews were descended from nomadic, desert tribes who settled in Palestine soon after 2000 BC. About 500 years later famine drove many of them to Egypt, where they lived as subjects of the Egyptians until Moses led them back to Palestine in about 1200 BC. By 1000 BC they had formed a single kingdom under King David, who made Jerusalem his capital. Later they fell under Assyrian and Babylonian rule, and in the 6th century BC most of the ablest people were carried off to exile in Babylon. The Persian conquest (539 BC) allowed them to return.

The story of the early history of the Jews is told in vivid language in the Bible.

For a time in the 2nd and 1st centuries BC there was an independent Jewish state, but it fell to the Romans in 63 BC.

About 100 years later the Jews rebelled against Roman rule. The rebellion was crushed and Jerusalem was destroyed (AD 70). Many Jews fled abroad, to join the Diaspora ('Dispersion' – Jews living in other countries). An independent Jewish state was not created again until 1948.

Moses led the Israelites from Egypt, through the desert, to the 'Promised Land' in Canaan (Palestine). Greatest of the Hebrew prophets and teachers, Moses was the chief founder of Judaism, the Jewish religion.

Right: In Palestine people might share their house with goats and donkeys. Most social life took place on the roof or outside, perhaps around the well.

*The kingdom of Heaven that Jesus described was a place of the spirit, not the proud, independent Jewish kingdom for which the Jews longed.*

## Christianity

The Jews believed in a Messiah, or Saviour, who would appear one day to lead them to freedom. One of several people who were thought to be the Messiah in Roman times was Jesus of Nazareth, a carpenter's son. However, Jesus preached love, tolerance and humility, which were not the qualities that the conservative Jewish leaders expected in the Messiah. At their insistence, the Romans put Jesus to death as a traitor (probably in AD 29).

Jesus's teaching lived on through his disciples, especially St Paul, and resulted in an altogether new religion, Christianity. With its all-powerful but all-forgiving God and its promise of a heavenly life after death, Christianity had a strong appeal for poor people. In spite of persecution, Christianity spread rapidly.

By the end of the 3rd century it was the strongest religion in the civilized, Roman world. It became organized as a Church, and Christian leaders began to collect written records of Jesus's life and teaching – the New Testament.

*Right: Jesus's life and works are recorded in four 'gospels' (meaning 'good news'). The earliest, St Mark's gospel, was written at least 30 years after Jesus's death. With the possible exception of Mark, none of the gospel writers had known Jesus in person.*

# The Roman Empire

Under Roman rule Europe enjoyed a long period of peace and prosperity. The empire continued to grow, up to the death of the Emperor Trajan. His successor, Hadrian, called a halt to conquest. Hadrian introduced a 'golden age' of Roman civilization, but by AD 200 the long decline had begun and Rome had to fight to defend its borders. The Emperor Constantine founded a second capital, Constantinople, in the East, but Rome itself eventually fell to the jealous 'barbarians' who invaded its borders. These invaders admired Rome and its civilization. They wanted to take it over themselves.

Hadrian's Wall, in northern England.

## War, law and language

The Roman empire was conquered, and then kept, by the army. The Roman army was the first with soldiers who were trained professionals. They were volunteers who signed on for 20 years of service and were well trained, armed and paid.

Besides fighting, they built roads, forts, defences (like Hadrian's Wall in northern Britain), and even towns. When they retired they received a pension. As an army, they were too good for the less well-disciplined forces of the Celts and other conquered peoples. They might lose a battle, but they seldom lost a war.

The empire was held together not only by the might of the Roman army, but by Roman law and the Romans' language, Latin, which was the common language of all educated Europeans until comparatively recent times. Roman law is the basis of the legal system in most Western countries today. It was generally fair, though severe. The Romans did not interfere too much with local customs as long as people obeyed the law and paid their taxes.

It was an advantage to be a Roman citizen. This gave a man a certain status, useful in trade or business deals, and inspired respect from officials. In later times, any free man could be a citizen. He did not have to be a Roman, or even an Italian. More than one Roman emperor was a 'foreigner'.

*A Roman country house, or villa. It was built around a central courtyard, or atrium, with a garden surrounded by a colonnade, like the cloisters of a monastery. From the outside it was plain, but inside it was luxurious, with rich wall paintings, mosaic floors and hot-air, under-floor central heating.*

| TIMETABLE | |
|---|---|
| AD | |
| 43 | Romans conquer Britain |
| 106 | Romans conquer Dacia (Romania) and Arabia |
| 117 | Romans conquer Armenia and Mesopotamia |
| 132 | Jewish rebellion against Rome |
| 212 | All free subjects of the empire awarded citizenship |
| 238 | Gothic invasions begin; rebellions now common |
| 313 | Christianity accepted by Constantine |
| 330 | Capital of the empire moved to Constantinople |
| 406–409 | Vandals rampage through Gaul and Spain |
| 410 | Alaric captures Rome |

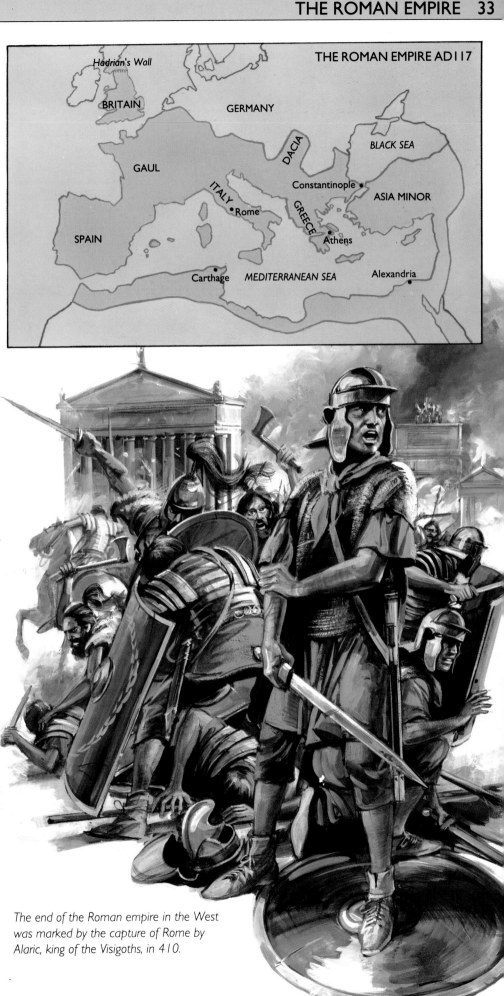

THE ROMAN EMPIRE AD 117

## Roman civilization

The empire contained people of many races, languages and religions, and its influence spread beyond its borders. The Romans themselves were the successors of the Greeks (and the Etruscans), and they were admirers of Greek literature, art and philosophy. Most works of art that decorated rich Roman houses were by Greek artists. Educated Romans spoke Greek as well as Latin.

Although they produced fine playwrights, poets and historians (including Julius Caesar himself), the finest qualities of the Romans were practical ones. They were better engineers than artists, and better lawyers than philosophers.

The Romans believed their empire would last for ever, and their buildings show it. To make them secure they built them stronger than necessary, and some buildings have lasted to this day: huge public buildings, such as the Colosseum in Rome as well as bridges, aqueducts and roads all over the empire. The drains and water supply in a Roman town were better than any European city possessed until the 19th century.

The end of the Roman empire in the West was marked by the capture of Rome by Alaric, king of the Visigoths, in 410.

# References

**Abraham** The legendary father-figure of the Jews, mentioned in the book of Genesis, in the Bible.

**Achmaenids** The name of the ruling dynasty of Persia from the 7th century BC to 331 BC.

**Aqueduct** A channel for carrying water, raised on stone arches like a bridge; the Roman aqueduct at Segovia, Spain, is still standing.

**Archaic period** The early period of Greek civilization, 800–500 BC.

**Archimedes** (died 212 BC) Greek mathematician and inventor who discovered the principle of the screw and the law that the loss of weight of a body in fluid equals the weight of the fluid it displaces.

**Aristotle** (384–322 BC) Greek philosopher, student of Plato, tutor of Alexander, who wrote learned works on a huge variety of scientific, literary and philosophical subjects.

**Bible** The holy book of Christianity, which consists of the Old Testament (the Jewish Bible) and the New Testament.

**Caesar** The name of a powerful Roman family, including Julius Caesar, which was adopted by Augustus and came to mean simply 'emperor'.

**Classical** A name given to both the whole period of Greek and Roman civilization and also to the peak period of Greek, especially Athenian, history, from about 500 to 300 BC.

**Colosseum** An amphitheatre in Rome (its ruins still stand), built in the 1st century AD for public entertainments; it could hold 80,000 people.

**Constantine** (died AD 337) Roman emperor from 306, who made Christianity legal and built a new capital, Constantinople, or Byzantium, in the East.

**Delian League** An alliance of Eastern Greek cities against Persia, formed in 478 BC and led by Athens, which became no more than an Athenian empire.

**Etruscans** An Italian people who developed a fascinating civilization in the region of Tuscany, northern Italy, in pre-Roman times.

**Famine** Shortage of food leading to widespread starvation, a common affliction in ancient times.

**Goths** A Germanic people, who migrated south and began to threaten the Roman empire in the early 3rd century AD; they were divided into Visigoths (west Goths) and Ostrogoths (east Goths). The Romans bribed them to go away, but in 410 the Visigoths captured Rome, and in the 5th century the king of the Ostrogoths made himself emperor.

**Hadrian** (AD 76–138) Roman emperor from 117, who secured the borders of the empire and was responsible for many of the finest Roman buildings.

**Hellenistic period** The name describing the Greek civilization spread over the Mediterranean world by Alexander the Great, from the 330s into Roman times.

**Justinian** (483–565) Byzantine, or Eastern emperor from 527, who briefly recovered some Roman possessions in Italy, Spain and North Africa, built many churches and monasteries, and compiled a collection of Roman laws, known as the Code of Justinian.

**Marathon** A town north-east of Athens, site of a famous victory over the Persians (490 BC), news of which was carried to the city by a runner (the origin of the modern marathon race).

**Moses** Hebrew prophet and lawgiver who introduced the Ten Commandments while leading his people out of Egypt in about the 13th century BC.

**Olympic games** The main athletic (at first, chiefly religious) festival of ancient Greece, supposed to have begun in 776 BC, a date used by the Greeks as the beginning of their calendar, and held every four years.

**Parchment** Animal skin, usually sheep or goat, prepared as a writing surface, like paper.

**Peloponnesian War** The great civil war in Greece which lasted from 431 to 404 BC.

**Persian Wars** The unsuccessful efforts of the Persians to conquer Greece (which had assisted the East Greek cities in their rebellion against Persian rule), between 490 and 479 BC.

**Plato** (died 347 BC) Greek philosopher, student of Socrates, especially famous for his work in political theory, *The Republic.*

**Prophet** Among the Hebrews, a godly man who taught God's will and often warned of future disaster if it were disobeyed.

**Ptolemy** (lived 2nd century AD) Alexandrian astronomer, mathematician and geographer, whose work was the basis of maps and atlases until the time of Columbus.

**Punic Wars** Wars between Rome and Carthage, 264–241, 218–201 and 149–146 BC, which ended with the complete destruction of Carthage.

**Semitic peoples** A name describing many peoples of the Middle East and North Africa, including the ancestors of the Arabs and Jews, whose native languages were related.

**Socrates** (died 399 BC) Greek philosopher, famous for the 'Socratic method' of teaching by question and answer, whose work is known only through the books of pupils, especially Plato.

**Trajan** (AD 52–117) Roman emperor (from AD 98) of Spanish birth, a great general who brought the empire to its greatest size by his wars in Dacia, Armenia and Parthia (Iran).

**Vandals** A Germanic people from eastern Europe who invaded the Roman empire early in the 5th century and, after rampaging through Gaul and Spain, eventually settled in North Africa.

# *Medieval Civilizations*

# China

For over a thousand years, up to modern times, China experienced periods of prosperity and high artistic achievement, followed by periods of weakness, bad government, rebellion and invasion. The basic values of Chinese civilization were never lost, however, thanks to the influence of Confucian beliefs and to a class of elite civil servants with a strong sense of tradition.

## T'ang

The T'ang dynasty (618–906) was founded by a successful general. It greatly expanded the Chinese frontiers by conquering much of Manchuria, Mongolia, Tibet and Turkestan, as well as Korea. China became the greatest empire in the world, and its capital, Chang-an, the world's largest city. The main avenue leading to the palace was 150m (500ft) wide. Trade flourished, especially in the south, which was becoming the Chinese heartland. The rivers were the main highways, and new towns appeared along their banks, but good roads were built, too. Trade caravans arrived regularly from central Asia, and Arabian ships called at the South China ports.

One sign of the new prosperity was a 'golden age' in the arts. But improvements even reached the hard-worked peasants in the countryside. Irrigation schemes, better livestock and crops, and successful battles against the menace of locusts made farming more productive. However, the power of big landlords prevented the government reorganizing land ownership, and it was a peasant rebellion that finally destroyed the failing power of the T'ang in the 9th century.

*Chinese cities were well planned, often as a rectangle divided into a grid of wide streets. Under the Sung they had street cleaning and lighting. They were crowded and lively, with fairs, markets, restaurants, tea houses and places of entertainment, as well as homes for orphans and old people.*

Above: *Pottery is one of the oldest and most skilled of Chinese crafts, exported from early times (giving us the name 'china'). The Chinese were the first to make true porcelain and the first to discover how to make silk, the most luxurious of textiles, from the fibres spun by the caterpillar of the silkworm moth to make its cocoon.*

Below: *Our word 'cash' comes from the strings of pierced copper coins used by the Chinese. By 1000 they were also using paper money.*

## Sung

The authority of the T'ang government gradually collapsed, ending in a period of chaos, the Five Dynasties. Even so, this was the time when printing began, with the characters carved in wooden printing blocks. China was rescued and reunited, though as a much smaller country, by the Sung dynasty in 960. Sung China was not a great military and imperial power like the T'ang, and the north was lost to the 'barbarian' Chin in 1126. The Southern Sung continued until 1279.

The Sung was a period of brilliance in the arts, such as landscape painting and calligraphy (handwriting).

Great cities arose: there were at least five with more than a million inhabitants each.

Gunpowder was in use, and a form of inoculation against smallpox was invented. In general, Chinese civilization was ahead of Europe. Even the 12 million Chinese peasants were probably a little better off than the peasants of Europe.

Another example of Chinese technological advance was in shipping. On land, they were surrounded by enemies, so the Sung were forced to look to the sea. They developed a navy and encouraged trade. Among other advantages, Chinese ships, called junks, were built with bulkheads (internal walls) dividing the hull into watertight compartments that could be sealed off from the rest of the ship.

## BUDDHISM

The Indian religion of Buddhism reached China in Han times (206 BC– AD 220) and became a powerful influence under the early T'ang, especially the formidable Empress Wu. Some of the world's first great travellers were Chinese Buddhist monks who went to India to consult early Buddhist writings. Buddhism did not clash with Confucian beliefs, nor with Taoism, nor the old Chinese religion of ancestor-worship. But in the 9th century, during a campaign against foreign religions, thousands of Buddhist temples and other treasures were destroyed. Buddhism was never again so strong in China, but it had already left its mark on Chinese civilization.

# The Mongols

Among the tribal peoples who constantly threatened Chinese civilization were the Mongols. The Chinese built the Great Wall to keep them out, but in the 13th century the Mongols broke out from the bleak plains of Mongolia to conquer most of Asia and part of eastern Europe. Under Genghis Khan they held the largest single empire (measured by area) that the world has seen, though it lasted only a few years.

## Mongol China

The conquest of China was completed by Kubilai Khan, a grandson of Genghis Khan, who ruled as emperor from 1279 to 1294. In theory he ruled, as the 'Great Khan', over the whole Mongol empire, but in reality he had little power outside China. His efforts to conquer Japan and other neighbours ended in failure, though he was able to extract large payments as the price for leaving them alone in future.

Kubilai was an intelligent man who admired Chinese culture. Apart from the destruction caused during his conquest, he interfered very little with Chinese life and customs, and saw himself more as a Chinese emperor than as a Mongol conqueror. He restored the city of Pekin (Beijing), making it the capital, and helped to expand Chinese trade and improve communications. He lent government ships to private merchants, and he organized the exploration of remote regions, trying to find the source of the Yellow River.

The successors of Kubilai were less able rulers, and the

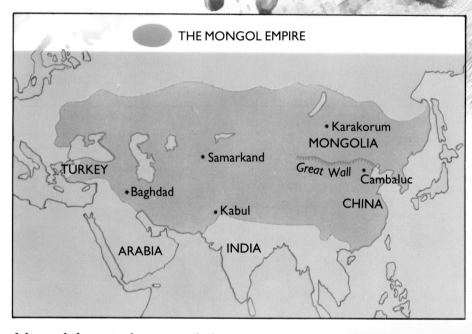

THE MONGOL EMPIRE

• Karakorum
MONGOLIA
• Samarkand
TURKEY
Great Wall • Cambaluc
• Baghdad
CHINA
• Kabul
ARABIA    INDIA

Mongol dynasty began to fail more quickly than most. By the middle of the 14th century, rebellions were breaking out everywhere. In 1368 the remaining Mongols fled the country.

Below: *The Mongols were a nomadic people. Each family carried a great round tent, called a ger or yurt, made of felt on a wooden frame.*

*Left: The Mongols were fine horsemen. They could fire their great bows while riding at full gallop. They also had giant catapults for attacking towns. They were cruel, but liked to be known as cruel as it made people more frightened of them.*

## Ming

The Ming was the last native Chinese dynasty (1368–1644), founded by the son of a peasant, Chu Yuan-chang. Although he left political power in the hands of landowners and officials, he ended the violence and made China a strong and wealthy state again. Trade with Europe was at a peak. Porcelain factories worked to meet European orders, including special commissions for dinner sets with the customer's coat of arms. The silk industry was equally profitable.

Chinese ships roamed the seas seeking more trade. On one of his voyages, the admiral Cheng Ho brought back a live giraffe from East Africa.

But the Chinese were suspicious and hostile toward foreigners. Ming officials were alarmed by the large number of foreigners in China, especially the Christian missionaries. Foreign voyages ceased, and the free movement of missionaries was stopped, though they were allowed to stay in Macao.

### TAMERLANE

The Mongol Khan Timur 'the Lame' (1336–1405) claimed that he was descended from Genghis Khan. He set up his capital at Samarkand and conquered most of the Middle East as well as southern Russia. In 1398 he attacked Delhi, in India, leaving his usual trademark – huge piles of human skulls – to mark his conquest.

Despite such deeds, Timur was an educated man and a devout Muslim, interested in science and the arts. He was an ancestor of the Mughal dynasty, which ruled India from the 16th century.

*Left: Unlike the Chinese, the Mongols were ready to welcome foreigners into their dominions. Italian merchants travelled to China and even to the Mongol capital, Karakorum. One, Marco Polo, spent 20 years in the service of Kubilai Khan.*

# Japan

Japan, a country of islands off the coast of Asia, has never been successfully invaded, and the Japanese were able to develop in their own way without foreign domination. Nevertheless, Japan was greatly influenced by the older civilization of its great neighbour, China.

## Clans and warlords

Although Japan could support a large population, thanks to fishing and rice-growing, it is a small and mountainous country. Shortage of land was another influence on Japanese history, while sea and mountains made it difficult for the central government to control the country. The Japanese emperors claimed descent from the goddess of the Sun, but they were almost powerless. Japan was divided up among a number of powerful clans and, at different times, one or other (like the Fujiwara in the 9th century) gained control of emperor and government. The leader was given the military title *shogun* and sometimes enjoyed the power of a dictator. In other periods, when the ruler was weak, power fell to the *daimyo*, the leaders of the warrior clans. They ruled as independent lords in their own district and made frequent war against their neighbours.

*Right: A samurai stands before a daimyo castle. Unlike European armour, which was fitted to the man who wore it, the armour of a Japanese warrior hung in plates of metal and leather, and sometimes included a frightening mask. The main weapon was a two-handed sword.*

*The Japanese love of strict form and ritual affected everyday life. Even tea-drinking became a ceremony.*

The shoguns and the daimyo represented the warlike side of Japanese society. This military tradition was strengthened by the need to defend the country against enemies, like the all-conquering Mongols, whose attacks were beaten off. The Japanese warrior, or *samurai*, whose life was ideally bound by honour, loyalty and simple living, was an important figure in Japanese society.

The principles of the samurai were connected with Zen Buddhism, which taught a life of prayer, meditation and closeness to nature, and rejected all forms of luxury. These traditions became a permanent influence on Japan, and they have not quite vanished today.

| RULING CLANS and SHOGUNATES | | |
|---|---|---|
| **Date** | **Period** | **Capital** |
| 710–784 | Nara Period | Nara |
| 794–1185 | Heian Period | Kyoto |
| 858–1156 | Fujiwara Clan | |
| 1192–1333 | Kamakura Shogunate | Kamakura |
| 1185–1219 | Minamoto Clan | |
| 1338–1568 | Ashikaga Shogunate | Kyoto |
| 1603–1867 | Tokugawa Shogunate | Yedo (Tokyo) |

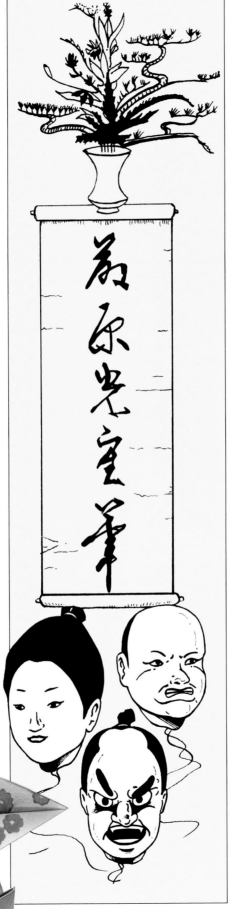

## Japanese culture

The Japanese developed unique art forms which, in their delicacy and refinement, make a strong contrast with the stern and simple approach to life of the samurai tradition. The spirit of Zen can be seen in their ink paintings of a single colour, and in Noh drama, which reached its peak in the 15th century. The Japanese had a knack of making an art of humble crafts, like landscape gardening (which was almost an outdoor form of ink painting) or paper folding. But a different spirit affected the Ashikaga shogun who built himself a lakeside villa covered with gold!

Chinese influence was strong. But representatives of another, very different civilization, first reached Japan in 1543. These were the 'southern barbarians', as the Japanese called Europeans. Among other things, they brought firearms, and the daimyo hastily began to rebuild their castles in stone. However, the days of the warlords were nearing an end. In 1563 a general named Nobunaga, commanding an army with guns, captured Kyoto (the capital) and began to reunite the nation. The task was completed by the Tokugawa shoguns, who were to expel the Europeans and rule Japan in isolation from the rest of the world until 1867.

Left: *Japanese arts and crafts included flower arranging, calligraphy and origami (paper folding). Masks were worn by actors in the Noh drama.*

# India

The subcontinent of India (which includes the modern countries of Pakistan and Bangladesh as well as India) is separated from the rest of Asia by mountain ranges. It can only be entered through a few mountain passes in the north-west. It was by that route that a long succession of invaders entered India. Most of them never reached the south.

## Maurya and Gupta empires

Soon after Alexander the Great's brief visit to north-west India, a king called Chandragupta created an empire in the valleys of the Ganges and Indus rivers. The most remarkable ruler of this dynasty was Asoka (273–232 BC), who was so shocked by the horrors of war that he became a peace-loving Buddhist. Buddhism was based on the teachings of Siddartha Gautama, Buddha, who lived in about 500 BC. He aimed to overcome the selfishness of the individual person by seeking the way to 'enlightenment' through good behaviour and meditation.

Hinduism was also developing at this time. While there were many conflicts between them, both Buddhism and Hinduism existed side by side in India for centuries.

Asoka ruled by the principles of *Dhamma* (roughly 'universal law'), and set up stone pillars engraved with his principles of government. He was also a practical reformer, planting banyan trees by the roads to provide shade for travellers.

The collapse of the Maurya empire in the 2nd century BC was followed by centuries of disunity, when many invaders brought in foreign influences. But in the 4th century AD northern India was reunited under the Gupta emperors. For over 200 years the region enjoyed a 'golden age'. Signs remain in marvellous stone temples, and in the literary classics of Sanskrit, the ancient language spoken throughout India. Hindu society was finally established in the Gupta period; in many ways it has changed little since.

Below: *Hindu temples are as much works of art as they are buildings. The Kailasanatha temple at Ellora, which dates from the 8th century, is really a gigantic piece of sculpture. It was carved from solid rock, starting at the top.*
Inset: *The god Shiva, dancing.*

*Above: In the countryside of India village life went on in much the same way for centuries. This scene from Gupta times would not be very different today.*

## Islam

Buddhism almost disappeared from India, but Hinduism grew stronger. Hinduism had a way of absorbing other beliefs, and it survived even the invasion of the powerful new influence of Islam.

Muslim armies had invaded India from Afghanistan for many years before the Islamic Delhi sultanate was founded in the late 12th century. The Delhi sultans dominated all India as far south as the Deccan, but this was not a national government like that of the Guptas. It included many Hindu states which, as long as they paid their taxes when required, were allowed to remain independent.

After the invading Timur and his Mongols ransacked Delhi and killed thousands of people in 1398, the sultanate never fully recovered its authority. Northern India broke up into small states ruled by quarrelsome princes, until the founders of a new Muslim dynasty, the Mughals, swept through the passes in the 16th century to create a spectacular new empire.

## THE CASTE SYSTEM

From ancient times Indian society was based on the caste system. The four main castes, or classes, were hereditary. It was almost impossible to move from one to another. The four main castes were Brahmins (priests and scholars), Kahatriyas (princes and warriors), Vaisyas (merchants and craftsmen), and Sudras (labourers). Many more existed, ending with the 'Outcastes', who were looked down on by everybody else.

Brahmin

Kahatriya

Vaisya

Sudra

# The Americas

The ancestors of the many peoples of the Americas crossed from Siberia into Alaska between 10,000 and 30,000 years ago. They spread throughout the two continents, following the animals they hunted. The last to arrive were probably the ancestors of today's Eskimo, or Inuit. Many different kinds of human society developed. Some remained in the Stone Age but, in Middle America (Mexico to Peru), civilizations arose – later than, but separate from, the civilizations of the Old World.

Large, rather threatening-looking stone heads were made by the Olmecs. No one knows their purpose.

## Mexico

The earliest American civilization was that of the Olmecs, who had settled in parts of Mexico before 1000 BC.

They were expert sculptors and modellers, and made use of rubber many centuries before it was known in Europe. We know very little about them, but just enough to see that the better-known civilization of the Maya must have developed from theirs.

Mayan civilization was at its height between about 500 and 900. The Maya were forest people who built great religious centres of vast stone temples, pyramids, tombs and terraces – without metal tools. Obviously, religion was very important in their lives, and their rulers were probably priests. To keep track of religious festivals, the Maya had a calendar which was based on very accurate observation of the movements of the stars. They understood a good deal about mathematics, including the concept of zero, and had a form of writing, using paper made from pressed plant fibres. Painted scenes of Maya life on plaster walls show rebellions of the peasant-farmers against their leaders, perhaps the cause of the civilization's decline.

From the 10th century the Maya centres fell into the hands of a warlike people from central Mexico, the Toltecs. Though not great originators themselves, they built some of the most impressive temples in America.

The Maya had to clear the forest to grow crops. The board on the baby's head and the dangling beads encouraged a sloping forehead and a squint – thought handsome by the Maya.

Ancient Mexican civilization continued under the Aztecs, the dominant people when the Europeans arrived in the 16th century. They lived by trade and conquest, and their capital city, Tenochtitlan, may have held 500,000 people. They worshipped many gods (headed by the Sun god), some of whom were extremely savage and demanded human sacrifices. But besides the violence of their religion and warfare, the Aztecs were good farmers (without ploughs, carts or draught animals), capable governors and fine craftsmen. We have some of their picture writing, made with great skill, patience and a powerful sense of design.

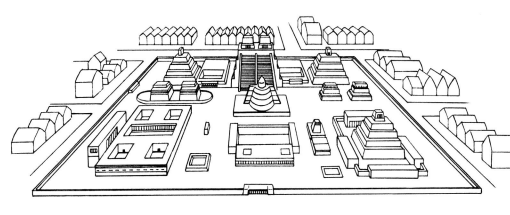

Above: *Tenochtitlan, the Aztec capital, was built on a lake and reached by a causeway. Towers and terraced gardens rose from broad streets and canals. The most impressive building was the temple of the Sun god, Huitzilopochtli, high on a pyramid.*

*The Inca city of Machu Picchu was built of stone, without mortar. The government messenger holds a quipu, a bunch of knotted cords carrying a coded message. The Incas had no written language.*

## The Incas

Civilization in Middle America reached its peak with the Incas, who ruled an empire of eight million people in Peru and Chile at the same time as the Aztecs, though no contact existed between them. Inca cities were built high in the Andes and connected by paved roads. In some ways, their government was surprisingly advanced. For example, a census was taken of the population; all produce belonged to the state and was shared out among the people; special arrangements were made for the sick and elderly. The Incas were tolerant towards the people they conquered, allowing them to continue their own customs instead of either killing them or making them slaves, as did the Aztecs. But in other ways, Inca government was as dictatorial as the Aztecs'. Society was divided into classes – nobles, workers and slaves – and private life was closely supervized. A blind man, for example, could only marry a blind woman.

# Africa

Europeans used to call Africa 'the dark continent', because they knew so little about it. Although North Africa had belonged to the Mediterranean world since ancient times and there was always some contact with lands farther south, most of Africa was cut off by the Sahara desert and the encircling sea. Large empires rose and fell in the Sahel region, but nothing was known about them outside Africa.

## Kingdoms and empires

By about the 10th century a single civilization existed in Africa from Senegal to the Red Sea, stretching as far south as Zimbabwe. It consisted of a large and often-changing collection of small kingdoms, ruled by kings who, like the ancient Egyptian pharaohs, were treated as gods. Sometimes, a group of them would collect around a powerful centre, then the 'empire' would break up again and new kingdoms form. The difficulties of farming in Africa, such as the lack of good native crops and the presence of pests like the tsetse fly, made a stable and peaceful life more difficult.

Trade routes crossed the Sahara from north to south, and the Saharan trade was partly responsible for the rise of much larger states in the western Sahel. The empire of Ghana (no relation to modern Ghana) gained its prosperity from its control of the trade in gold from the south and salt from the north. Founded by Berbers from North Africa in the 4th century, it reached its height under the black rulers who took over in the 8th century.

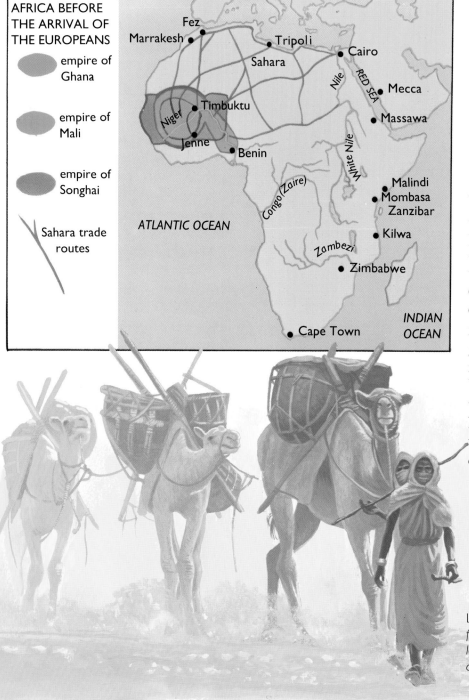

AFRICA BEFORE THE ARRIVAL OF THE EUROPEANS

empire of Ghana

empire of Mali

empire of Songhai

Sahara trade routes

Fez
Marrakesh
Tripoli
Sahara
Cairo
Nile
RED SEA
Mecca
Massawa
Niger
Timbuktu
White Nile
Jenne
Benin
Congo (Zaire)
Malindi
Mombasa
Zanzibar
ATLANTIC OCEAN
Kilwa
Zambezi
Zimbabwe
INDIAN OCEAN
Cape Town

Left: *Trade caravans crossed the Sahara from Roman times. The desert was slightly less dry then, and the use of camels (from about the 4th century) made travel easier.*

In the 13th century Ghana was replaced by the larger empire of Mali, whose rulers soon became Muslims (this made life easier for black African merchants trading in Muslim North Africa). This was a well-governed empire, with little crime or violence, but was weakened by the attacks of the nomadic Tuareg in the 14th century and eventually taken over by the Songhai, formerly its subjects.

The Songhai empire, larger still, had its capital at Gao, but its authority rested mainly on military strength, which is seldom a sound basis for government. Songhai control of the Saharan trade aroused jealousy in the north, and in 1591 the Songhai were overthrown by the forces of the sultan of Morocco.

A West African village. Most of the hard work was done by the women. Craftsmen such as blacksmiths and carvers of gods and ancestor-figures had special status in the community.

Below: Muslim port-cities like Kilwa, Malindi, Mombasa and Zanzibar were busy international centres of Indian Ocean trade (in ivory, cloth, and other goods) from the 13th century.

### East Africa

As early as the 4th century a Christian missionary from Syria reached Ethiopia by travelling up the Nile. As a result a Christian kingdom was created which, protected by mountains, continued to exist in the middle of what became a Muslim region. It lasted into this century.

Farther south, Muslim traders from the Red Sea and Arabian Gulf created little city-states on the coast where a unique Afro-Arab society developed, with a new language, Swahili. Still farther south and inland lay the African state of Zimbabwe, the ruins of whose ceremonial buildings, over 500 years old, can still be seen. Little is known of this state, which gained its wealth from the gold trade.

# References

**Afghanistan** A mountainous, tribal country from which came most of the invasions of India; often subject to foreign domination, it was not united until the 18th century.

**Andes** The mountains which stretch along the western side of South America.

**Bantu** A name used to describe the African peoples, speaking similar languages, who spread over most of Africa south of the equator.

**Benin** A major West African state from the 13th century (in 1602 its capital reminded a Dutch visitor of Amsterdam), famous also as a centre of ancient African art, especially bronzes.

**Berbers** The native people of northern Africa (including the Tuareg) who resemble Arabs and were often confused with them.

**Brahmanism** The early form of the Hindu religion; Brahmans dominated the intellectual side of Hinduism and produced much of its literature, including the *Vedantas*.

**Bunraku** Japanese puppet theatre, a unique form of drama. *See also* **Kabuki, Noh drama.**

**Chichen Itza** A great Mayan religious 'city' in Yucatan, Mexico, containing pyramid-temples 1 acre in area, decorated with sculptures and paintings.

**Deccan** The central plain of India.

**Delhi sultanate** The first Muslim empire in India, in the 13th and 14th centuries, which at its height stretched to the south of the Deccan.

**Genji, Tale of** The most famous work of Japanese literature, describing court life and written about 1000 (in Chinese) by the Lady Murasaki.

**Ghaznevids** A Muslim dynasty of Turkic people, based in Afghanistan from the late 10th to late 12th century, whose greatest ruler was Mahmud of Ghazni.

**Great Wall** Chinese defence against invasion by nomadic tribes, begun over 2,000 years ago.

**Huns** A nomadic people related to the Mongols who conquered much of northern Asia and eastern Europe, reaching their peak under Attila in the mid 5th century.

**Jainism** The third great native religion of India (with Hinduism and Buddhism), dating from the 4th century BC or earlier. Jains believe that earthly creatures are reborn many times in different forms and therefore take care not to harm any living thing.

**Junk** General name for Chinese seagoing ships, solid, squarish, slow but safe, with watertight compartments and sails reinforced with wooden strips.

**Kabuki** Traditional Japanese drama, originally mostly dancing, freer in form than Bunraku or Noh.

**Khan** A title meaning 'lord' or 'prince', used by the Mongols and later by other Asian peoples.

**Korea** The country forming a peninsula of eastern Asia, between China and Japan, which preserved its own identity in spite of domination by China, until the 13th century, and later by Japan.

**Macao** A small coastal region of China, occupied by the Portuguese in the 16th century and, with Canton, the only Chinese port open to European trade in the 18th–19th centuries.

**Noh drama** Traditional form of Japanese drama, very stylized in form, slow-moving, with simple plot, chanting, and masked actors.

**Old World** Europe and Asia (sometimes Africa also), in contrast with the 'New World' of the Americas.

**Porcelain** The finest form of ceramics (pottery), so delicate it allows light to pass through, first made in Europe in the 18th century but made in China nearly 1,000 years earlier.

**Sahel** The broad belt of land, mainly grassland, across Africa south of the desert and north of the forest.

**Shinto** The traditional Japanese religion, based on Nature and ancestor-worship, which after some early conflict with Buddhism adopted many Buddhist beliefs.

**Silk** Material woven from thread produced by silkworms (caterpillars of the silkworm moth), made over 4,000 years ago by the Chinese, who kept the secret for centuries.

**Sri Vijaya** One of several 'Hinduized' kingdoms of south-east Asia; its ships dominated trade in the Indian Ocean from the 8th to the 12th century.

**Tenochtitlan** The capital city of the Aztecs, where Mexico City is now, which was built on an island in a lake.

**Tsetse fly** The insect that causes sleeping sickness, a disease afflicting cattle and other animals as well as people in Africa.

**Tuareg** A pastoral-nomadic people of the Sahara, often a menace to towns and villages up to the 19th century, today sadly persecuted and few in number.

**Vedanta** A system of beliefs written during the Gupta period in India, in which material things are unimportant compared with the world of the spirit.

**Wu, Empress** (died 704) Chinese ruler of the T'ang dynasty, who succeeded in gaining the throne for herself after the death of her husband, the emperor.

**Yuan dynasty** The Mongol dynasty of Chinese emperors founded by Kubilai Khan.

**Zen Buddhism** A branch of Buddhism which appealed especially to scholars, warriors and nobles, teaching the way to 'enlightenment', or knowledge of the self, through strict discipline and meditation.

# The Medieval West

# The Franks

After the collapse of Roman rule in Western Europe, a number of 'barbarian' kingdoms were set up, but most soon disappeared again. An exception was the kingdom of the Franks, a tribal people who were settled in the region of the River Rhine in the 3rd century AD. In about 486 they were united under a Christian leader, Clovis, who, supported by the Roman Church against other Germanic tribes, conquered most of Gaul. Clovis's kingdom was more like a collection of family estates than a single state, and after his death it was divided among his sons. In the 8th century it was reunited to form a new 'Roman empire' by one of the greatest leaders in European history.

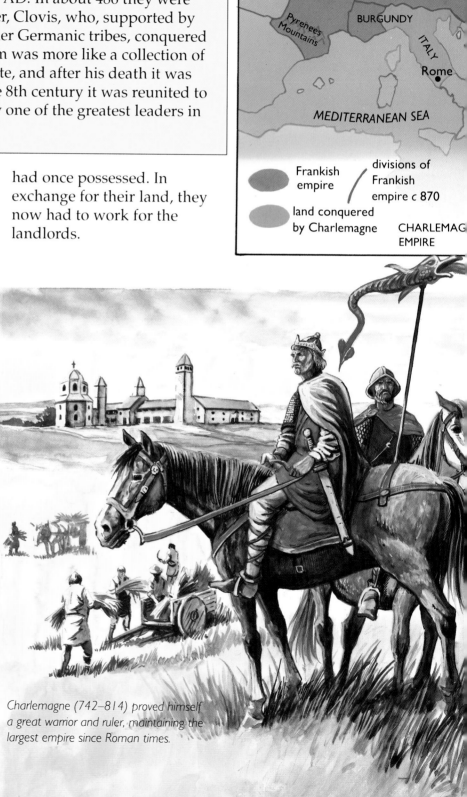

BRITAIN

Aachen

WEST FRANKS

EAST FRANKS

Pyrenees Mountains

BURGUNDY

ITALY

Rome

MEDITERRANEAN SEA

Frankish empire

divisions of Frankish empire c 870

land conquered by Charlemagne

CHARLEMAG EMPIRE

## Charlemagne

Charlemagne ('Charles the Great') was the grandson of Charles Martel ('the Hammer'), the Frankish leader who defeated the invading Muslims at the Battle of Poitiers in 732. During his reign (768–814) Charlemagne fought countless wars against Lombards, Saxons, Byzantines, Serbs, Bretons, Danes and Spanish Muslims. He created, and was able to maintain, the largest empire seen since Roman times.

Compared with the Muslim caliph's court in Baghdad, or the Byzantine court in Constantinople, the empire of Charlemagne was poor and backward. Trade, for example, seems to have been very small, and most contacts with the East had been broken by the recent Arab conquests in the Middle East.

The land was held mostly by large landowners, who included monasteries. Ordinary peasant-farmers were losing the freedom they had once possessed. In exchange for their land, they now had to work for the landlords.

*Charlemagne (742–814) proved himself a great warrior and ruler, maintaining the largest empire since Roman times.*

## CHARLEMAGNE

On Christmas Day 800, Charlemagne was crowned Roman Emperor by the Pope. There is some doubt if the Pope put the crown on his head or if Charlemagne crowned himself. This was important: did the Pope have authority over the emperor, or the emperor over the Pope? The question was to cause great difficulties in later centuries.

*Right: Scribes at work in the scriptorium or 'writing room' at Aachen. They copied Classical works as well as bibles and other religious books, using a script known as Carolingian minuscule, which spread throughout medieval Europe.*

## The Carolingian Renaissance

Charlemagne's duties as king were more than those of a great warrior. His court at Aachen, which he chose as his capital because of its warm springs in which he liked to bathe, became the centre of learning and art, attracting Arab and Jewish scholars as well as monks and priests from all over the Christian world. This 'renaissance', or rebirth, of scholarship was all the more remarkable because Charlemagne himself, for all his wisdom, ability and love of learning, could only write with some difficulty.

## 'French' and 'Germans'

Among the Franks, an estate was divided equally among a man's sons, and the empire of Charlemagne was divided into three by the Treaty of Verdun (843). Two of the three divisions, which were ruled by Charlemagne's grandsons, roughly corresponded to modern France and Germany. Both the French and the Germans claim Charlemagne as one of the founders of their country.

The idea of a single, Christian empire did not die with Charlemagne. Among his later successors was a German dynasty which, in the person of Otto I, revived the idea of a Holy (meaning 'Christian') Roman Empire. Otto succeeded in uniting the crowns of Germany and Italy and he was crowned as Holy Roman Emperor by the Pope in 962. The title was to last until the 19th century.

*The Emperor Otto I cooperated with the Church, but he regarded bishops as his own officials and expected them to be loyal to him before the Pope.*

# The English

The ancestors of the English were Germanic invaders, including Angles and Saxons, who settled in the south and east of England between the 5th and 6th centuries. By 600 they controlled most of England plus south-east Scotland, driving the earlier, Celtic inhabitants into the far north and west. The Anglo-Saxon tribes gradually formed a number of small kingdoms. These were united under the kings of Wessex after Wessex had taken the lead in defending England against the Vikings.

*The Anglo-Saxons were converted to Christianity by St Augustine of Canterbury, a missionary from Rome who arrived in 597.*

## Alfred the Great

Though King Alfred of Wessex (reigned 871–899) never ruled all England, he was the true founder of the English kingdom. He stood alone against the Vikings from Denmark, fought them to a draw and allowed them to settle in eastern England. He set up defensive burghs, or fortified towns, and built a navy to defend the country from future attack.

Like Charlemagne, he set himself the task of establishing a system of law, educating the people (or at least the sons of free men), and raising intellectual standards. It was Alfred, for example, who was responsible for starting the *Anglo-Saxon Chronicle*.

Alfred's immediate successors, including his daughter Aethelflaed of Mercia, were also strong and energetic rulers. They established their authority as (in the words of one of them) 'king of the English and' – this part was more doubtful – 'all the nations round about'. Later kings were weaker, but with one short interval of rule by Danish kings, the House of Wessex held the throne of England until the next successful invasion, by the Normans in 1066.

*Below: An Anglo-Saxon village.*

*King Alfred inspects the ships of the first English navy.*

## Wales and Scotland

Wales and Scotland were never conquered by the Anglo-Saxons. The Welsh kept their own Celtic language, law and form of Christianity, but, except for one short period, they were not united. After a long struggle, Wales became part of the English kingdom in the 13th century.

The Scots came originally from northern Ireland, and settled in the region of Argyll. In 843 their king, Kenneth McAlpin, made himself king of the native Picts and created a small Scottish kingdom. His successors gained Lothian from the English in 1018, inherited the kingdom of Strathclyde, and conquered the Norwegian possessions in the north and west. The Northern Isles were not gained from Norway until 1468.

## THE CELTS

The Celts were an Iron Age people who, in about 500 BC, began to spread west from central Europe, creating settled societies in Gaul, Britain and Ireland. They were warriors and farmers, with a powerful class of priests-lawkeepers called druids. The last wave of Celtic migrants were the Belgae, who gave Belgium its name and also moved into Britain. It was partly to stop the Britons helping their fellow Celts against Roman rule that the Romans invaded Britain. The Celts were fine metalworkers, with a marvellous sense of design, but although advanced in some ways (they are said to have been the first Europeans to wear trousers), their weapons were not so good as the weapons of Germanic tribes like the Saxons.

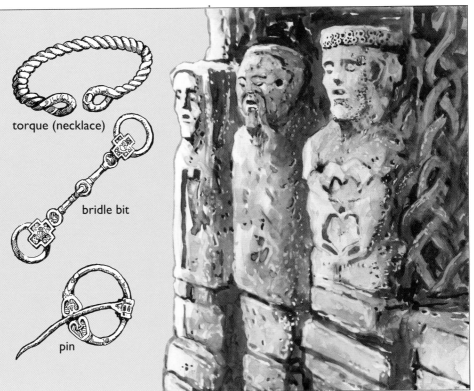

torque (necklace)

bridle bit

pin

# The Vikings

In the 8th century Western Europe came under attack from a new direction, from Scandinavia. The Vikings ('sea-warriors') included Danes, Norsemen (Norwegians) and Swedes. The main reason for their raids on neighbouring lands was probably shortage of farming land in Scandinavia for, although they were seen as pirates and robbers, they were also settlers and colonists. The kings of the English and the Franks reluctantly granted the invaders land. The Norsemen conquered Ireland, almost destroying its ancient Celtic civilization, and founded colonies in Iceland and Greenland (and, for a few years, in North America).

## Scandinavian voyages

The Vikings travelled amazing distances. The Danes raided Mediterranean coasts. Swedes went east, and settled at Novgorod and Kiev. One band went south to the Black Sea and attacked Constantinople; others reached Baghdad. The Norsemen crossed the North Atlantic, founding a new nation in Iceland and colonies in Greenland. They reached North America, visiting Newfoundland and perhaps Maine, though they were soon driven out by the local people.

The Vikings made excellent ships. In their speedy, square-sailed longships they raided European coasts, but they also built larger vessels with more room to carry families, with their possessions and food, for long voyages across a dangerous ocean.

However, Viking ships, though better made, were not so very different from the ships of ancient times. They still had no rudder or magnetic compass, and were steered with a large oar at the stern. The longships were ideal for raids in shallow waters, but in a naval battle they were no match for the larger ships of other European sea powers, which had raised 'castles' from which archers could shoot down at the rowers in the longships.

The Scandinavian longship was built for speed, and relied more on oars than sail. It carried up to 100 men, who probably rowed in three shifts, and was light enough to be carried overland by its crew if necessary. They also built smaller ships (knorrs), which they used for trading.

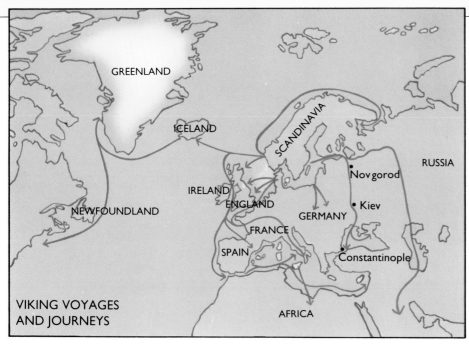

VIKING VOYAGES
AND JOURNEYS

## Scandinavian civilization

The Scandinavians were never mere thieves and raiders. In Ireland they built the first towns, including Dublin. In north and east England they soon settled down as farmers and traders. They were fine craftsmen, especially in metalwork, and in Iceland they produced a stirring form of national literature, the sagas. They also became Christians without too much fuss, and the fierce old Scandinavian gods, like Thor, who struck down giants and monsters by hurling his massive hammer, were forgotten – or, at least, no longer worshipped.

When the Scandinavians became Christians, in the 10th and 11th centuries, they also became less threatening. As they were drawn into European civilization, they lost some of their spirit of individual freedom. Still, their vigour and confidence were passed on to their descendants, especially the Normans. The leader of the Scandinavians who settled in Normandy was Ganger Rolf, a tremendous chieftain who was so big no horse could be found to carry him. He was a very different sort of ruler from Duke William of Normandy, who conquered England 150 years later, but both were formidable leaders and warriors.

Above: *Part of the agreement made between King Alfred and the Danish leader Guthrum in 878, which allowed the Danes to settle in eastern England, was that Guthrum should become a Christian.*

Below: *A Scandinavian home in Ireland in the 10th century. The Scandinavians were keen traders; some had settled peacefully in the British Isles before the Viking raids began.*

# The Norman Age

Since prehistoric times, Europe had been subjected to invasion by large bands of people seeking new territory. With the end of the Viking raids in the 11th century, that period came to an end, although Europe did not suddenly become peaceful. Men were still hungry for land, which meant power and riches. Europe was becoming a continent of kingdoms, but kings were not always the most powerful men around. The heads of great families sometimes held more land, and commanded more men, than the king. A ruler's success was still measured by conquest, and the most successful rulers of the age were the dukes of Normandy, who conquered England in 1066 and also created a kingdom for themselves in southern Italy.

## Feudalism

The way in which society was organized between the 11th and 14th centuries is called feudalism, a name which comes from a Latin word meaning a piece of land. Feudalism was not a universal system with strict rules, and it varied from one region to another, sometimes from one village to another. However, the main principle was simple: a man held his land from a landlord, and in return gave him service of some kind, especially military service.

In theory, all land was 'owned' by the king. He leased most of it to the great lords or barons, who swore loyalty and promised to support him in war (a promise often broken). The barons leased out estates in their turn to lesser lords, who swore loyalty to them.

*A Norman castle. A castle was something like a police station, from which law and order could be enforced on the surrounding country. The Normans were great builders of cathedrals and monasteries, too.*

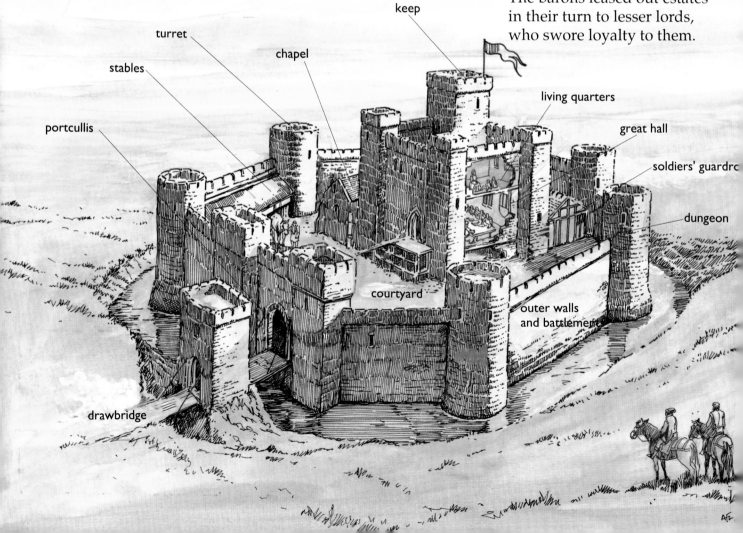

keep

turret

chapel

stables

living quarters

portcullis

great hall

soldiers' guardrc

dungeon

courtyard

outer walls
and battlemen

drawbridge

A feudal estate, sometimes called a lordship or manor, was often roughly the same as a village, with its surrounding land. Local government, including law enforcement and services like a mill to grind the corn, was provided by the landlord or his local steward. Some land was kept for the landlord, and the rest belonged to the peasants, or serfs, who were required to work on the lord's portion and perhaps give up part of their own crop.

## People and land

Serfs were not slaves, but they were not free men. For example, they could not leave the manor or choose a wife without the lord's permission. They could graze their animals and gather firewood on the common land, but they were not allowed to hunt game. Large areas were reserved for hunting – but for king and nobles only. Serfs could grind their corn at the lord's mill, but paid for it with a proportion of the flour. Although everyone worked on the land, the manor also had its craftsmen, such as blacksmiths, carpenters, wheelwrights and millers, for each little community supported itself. Few things were bought from outside and there were no real shops, only regular fairs in market towns.

Life was hard for everyone, but especially for the serfs. They seldom ate meat and a poor harvest meant famine. In bad times they ate nettle soup and bread made from ground acorns.

Above: *Part of the Bayeux Tapestry, a piece of embroidery about 70m long and 50cm wide, made between 1066 and 1077. It tells, in pictures, how, under Duke William, 'the Conqueror', the Normans crossed the English Channel and defeated the last Saxon king of England, Harold, at the Battle of Hastings in 1066.*

Below: *The Norman style of building is called 'Romanesque'. In the Roman manner, they built for strength, with thick stone walls and narrow, rounded arches. The Gothic style, which first appeared in the 12th century, was more open and delicate. It was based on the new principle of the pointed arch, which allowed a much larger space between walls or columns.*

Right: *The Domesday Book was a survey of property compiled in 1086 to provide a basis for taxation.*

# The Church

The most powerful authority in medieval Europe was not a kingdom or dukedom, it was the Christian Church, ruled by the Pope in Rome. The Church owned huge estates in every country. It controlled education and learning, and the parish priest was often the only person in a village who could read. His sermons were the sole source of news about the outside world. The Church was organized in a hierarchy, and priests existed at all levels of society, from royal court to humble village. It had its own system of law, which was enforced in Church courts.

## Monasteries

There were two kinds of clergy, priests and monks. The monasteries, especially those belonging to the 'order' or Rule of St Benedict, were centres of civilization in the countryside. Monks spent much time praying, but they also farmed the land and cared for the sick. Some were scholars and teachers, who spread the knowledge of Christianity throughout the land.

Although women could not be priests, they could become nuns, and they had their own religious houses, called convents. Like monks, they swore to obey strict rules of obedience, poverty and chastity.

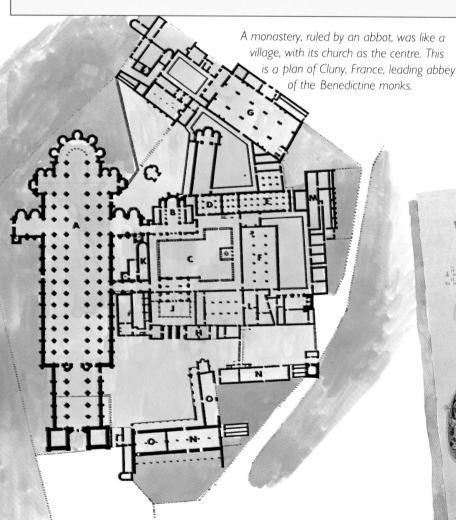

*A monastery, ruled by an abbot, was like a village, with its church as the centre. This is a plan of Cluny, France, leading abbey of the Benedictine monks.*

*One valuable task done by monks was to make copies of religious books. One man could spend many years producing the beautiful 'illuminations' (pictures) of a single manuscript.*

| | | | |
|---|---|---|---|
| A | abbey church | H | abbot's palace |
| B | third church | J | church with courtyard |
| C | cloisters | K | chapel |
| D | chapter house | L | kitchen |
| E | dormitory | M | latrines |
| F | refectory | N | stables |
| G | infirmary | O | guest house |

## The papacy

As head of the Church the Pope had great power and influence, but he did not have an army. He needed an ally or 'protector' who did. In the early Christian centuries, the Pope had looked to the Byzantine emperor in Constantinople, but by the 8th century, the Byzantine emperor had no power in Italy. The coronation of Charlemagne in 800 marked a new alliance between Church and State, or Pope and emperor, which was continued under Otto and the German kings, who revived the title of Holy Roman Emperor.

The Pope held religious authority over not only the clergy, but all people, including kings and emperors. But rulers considered themselves supreme in their own lands. This conflict of authority, between the religious power of the Church and the political power of states, caused grave problems. An example was the Investiture Conflict – a quarrel between the Pope and the emperor over who had the right to appoint (and therefore control) bishops.

The papacy reached the height of its power under Innocent III. But signs of its future decline had already appeared. A few small groups broke away from the authority of the Pope altogether, and the Inquisition was founded in Rome to root out heretics. Many people believed that the papacy was becoming too political. In 1305 the papacy moved from Rome to Avignon, in France. It was hard then to see the Pope as the supreme authority in Christendom. He looked more like the agent of the king of France. Finally, after the papacy had returned to Rome (1377), rivalry broke out over who was rightfully Pope. At one time three men claimed the title!

vaulting

flying buttresses

Coutances Cathedral in France is a fine example of early Gothic church architecture, built between 1200 and 1250.

### MURDER IN CANTERBURY

The English King Henry II quarrelled with the Archbishop of Canterbury, Thomas Becket, over the rights of English priests to be tried in church courts, not royal courts. In 1170 three of Henry's knights, without his knowledge, murdered Becket in Canterbury Cathedral. Yet Becket was the real victor in this quarrel. Henry stopped his campaign against the rights of the clergy, and walked to Canterbury as a pilgrim to show his repentance.

# The Byzantine Empire

Under the Emperor Justinian in the 6th century, the East Roman, or Byzantine empire stretched as far as Spain and Persia, and included much of Italy. Most of this was lost in the next century, when the Byzantine state might have disappeared altogether but for the campaigns of a great general and (later) emperor, Heraclius. Byzantium was surrounded by enemies, the greatest of whom were the forces of Islam – the Arabs in the 7th century, and later the Turks. During the long struggle with Islam, the Byzantine empire sometimes grew, sometimes shrank. After its defeat at Manzikert in 1071, it was no longer a great power. The empire shrank to almost nothing, and Constantinople itself fell in 1453, marking the end of an era.

An artist making a mosaic, an art that was highly developed in Byzantium.

## The Byzantine state

The Byzantine emperors saw themselves as direct successors to the emperors of ancient Rome, and never gave up the idea of rebuilding the old Roman empire under their rule. Although this may now seem an absurd ambition, it did not seem impossible to someone living in the rich and magnificent city of Constantinople, the largest city in Europe.

The Byzantine emperors were also the guardians of Christianity. The emperor's role was as head of the Church, and he was often pictured wearing a halo. There was no high priest, like the Pope in the West, able to challenge his absolute authority. Partly because the Byzantine people would not accept the papacy, the Christian Church eventually split into two separate factions, Roman (Western) and Orthodox (Eastern).

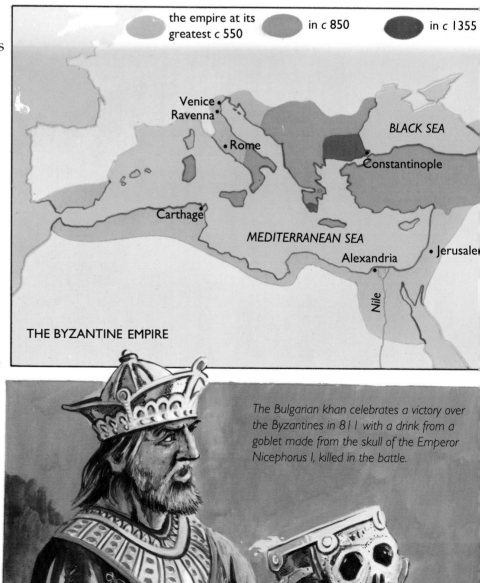

the empire at its greatest c 550    in c 850    in c 1355

Venice
Ravenna
Rome
BLACK SEA
Constantinople
Carthage
MEDITERRANEAN SEA
Alexandria
Jerusalem
Nile

THE BYZANTINE EMPIRE

The Bulgarian khan celebrates a victory over the Byzantines in 811 with a drink from a goblet made from the skull of the Emperor Nicephorus I, killed in the battle.

Perhaps the greatest of the debts owed to Byzantium was Justinian's Code of Law.

From the 11th century, the Byzantine empire was in decline, and its last small possessions in Italy fell to the Normans.

But at Constantinople, behind the huge city walls, little seemed to change. The 11th and 12th centuries were a period of great cultural achievement, and the city was as splendid as ever. But the old courageous fighting spirit had gone. The shrinking empire lacked enough subjects to make up a decent army, so foreign mercenaries had to be hired to defend it. The most surprising thing about the fall of Constantinople is that it did not happen earlier.

## Byzantine civilization

Byzantine civilization became very complicated, partly because it was influenced by many different traditions, Eastern as well as Western. The successors of Justinian were harassed by economic problems, religious quarrels and administrative difficulties of a kind which gave a new twist to the word 'Byzantine' – meaning extremely devious and complex.

Constantinople was a great centre of scholarship, and much of the ancient Greek literature that we know today was preserved by Byzantine scholars. Yet the Byzantines, though some of them were very learned, were also extremely conservative. They had little interest in new ideas in literature, art or other subjects. Nevertheless, Byzantium influenced the West in many ways. For example, the flat, almost abstract style of Byzantine art had an effect as far away as Celtic Ireland.

Below: *Byzantine traditions continued among the Slav nations of eastern Europe. The Russians adopted Orthodox Christianity after a sister of the Emperor Basil II married Prince Vladimir of Kiev. The glories of Byzantine religious worship can be witnessed today in the churches of Kiev or Moscow.*

# Muslim Conquests

In the 7th century a great new power appeared in the world. It was inspired by one man, Muhammad, a religious prophet and reformer in Arabia who became the founder of the Muslim religion. In 622 (the first year of the Muslim calendar) he and his followers fled from Mecca, where his preaching had made him many enemies, to Medina. He returned in triumph eight years later and by the time of his death (632), all Arabia was united in the worship of Allah, the one true god, and in recognizing Muhammad as his prophet. The Arabs then set out to conquer and convert the rest of the world.

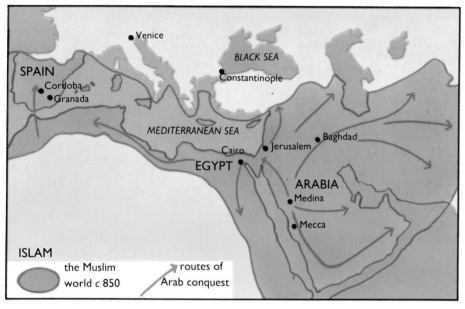

ISLAM
the Muslim world c 850    routes of Arab conquest

by the Abbasids, whose main support lay farther east. They moved the caliphate from Damascus to Baghdad (Iraq). The army, which had been led by Arabs, became a force of trained slaves, mainly Turkish. The Abbasid caliphate reached its peak in the reign of Harun al-Rashid (786–809). After that, weakness set in, partly as a result of internal divisions, especially between Arabs and Persians. The caliph's authority was reduced until his rule meant little beyond Iraq. Other dynasties, which were in practice independent, were set up in North Africa and Spain. The Fatimids, who ruled Egypt, even captured Baghdad for a short time.

## The Arab conquests

This astonishing breakout by a little-known, mainly nomadic people was an Arab nationalist movement as well as a religious crusade. In a few years, the Arabs had conquered Syria, Iraq, Iran and Egypt. Damascus became their capital and there the caliph, the political and religious head of Islam, had his court. Arab rule was welcomed in many countries, as the Arabs were tolerant of local customs and willing to employ people of other races and religions in their service. The Arabs were used to mixing with different peoples. The towns of Arabia before the conquests contained Jews, Christians, Persians and others. From the countries they conquered, the Arabs soon absorbed other traditions, which were often more advanced than their own.

For about 100 years, the Umayyad dynasty ruled the Arab–Muslim empire from Damascus (Syria), but in 750 the caliphate was taken over

ISLAM EXPANDS, 632–850

A romantic account of the court of Harun al-Rashid appears in the stories known as *The Arabian Nights*. Gorgeous carpets and gold vessels decorated the palace. Mechanical birds made of precious metals perched in artificial trees and sang. Scholars and poets came from far and wide to see the beautiful women of the court and to enjoy the caliph's hospitality. Al-Rashid was also a great warrior, who defeated the Byzantines and was only checked by the walls of the city of Constantinople itself.

*Mecca is the holiest of the holy cities of Islam, containing the sacred shrine known as the Kaaba. All Muslims turn towards Mecca when they pray and, if they can, make a pilgrimage to the holy city.*

## Islam

In spite of political divisions, Islam was a single civilization. The greatest contribution of the Arabs, after their religion, was their language, a rich and poetic one. Arabic became the universal language of educated Muslims, much as Latin had become the common language of Europe. Muslim law was based on the word of god as revealed to Muhammad in the Quran (Koran), the Holy Book of Islam.

The Arabs, with their ability to learn from different traditions, made many contributions to mathematics and science, and the most learned men of the early Middle Ages were Arab scholars like al-Idrisi. In art and architecture, new styles arose which were based partly on Greek, Roman and Byzantine traditions as well as on Eastern ones. In most ways, civilization in the Muslim-ruled part of Spain was ahead of the civilization of Christian Europe.

*Travel within the Islamic world was easy for Muslims, because of their shared religion. A great traveller named Ibn Batuta, a Moroccan, visited places as far apart as West Africa and Siberia in the 14th century.*

# The Crusades

It is difficult today, even for Christians, to understand the intense religious feeling which reached its height in the 12th century – when someone eating an apple would cut it into three parts in memory of the Holy Trinity. This religious enthusiasm found one outlet in wars against heretics and non-Christians. The main object of the Crusades, or wars of the Cross, was to reclaim the Holy Land (Palestine) from Muslim rule. For a short time, this effort was successful, but as the crusading spirit faded and Muslim resistance strengthened, the 'Crusader States' were lost. There were lesser crusades, more successful, like the wars of Christians against Muslims in Spain and the crushing of Albigensian heretics in southern France.

*A crusader and (below left) the Crusader castle of Krak des Chevaliers.*

Crusader states | Byzantine territory

ASIA MINOR (Seljuk Turks)

CYPRUS

Edessa
Antioch

MEDITERRANEAN SEA

Tripoli

Krak des Chevaliers

Acre

Damascus

Jerusalem

EGYPT

THE CRUSADES

## The First Crusade

Palestine had been in Muslim hands for 400 years before the victory of the Seljuk Turks at Manzikert (1071). After this defeat, the Byzantine emperor asked for help from his Western rival, the Pope. The Pope took up the cause, and in 1097 the First Crusade arrived in Constantinople. The Byzantine emperor had asked for military aid, not for several armies led by great French barons like the Duke of Normandy and the French king's brother. Relations between 'Greeks' (Byzantines) and 'Franks' (crusaders) were not easy: East and West had drifted too far apart in earlier centuries.

However, the First Crusade was a surprising success. The crusaders defeated the Turks and captured Jerusalem, killing the inhabitants. They did not return all the land they conquered to the Byzantine emperor, but set up new states, including a kingdom of Jerusalem ruled by a French prince. The loss of one of these new states in 1144 was the reason for the Second Crusade, which was a complete failure.

## The Third Crusade

In 1174 the Muslim leader known to Christians as Saladin gained control of Egypt and managed to unite the Muslims of the Middle East in a holy war (*jihad*) against the Christians. The Third Crusade (1190) was Europe's response to Saladin's capture of Jerusalem. It was led by great men – the Holy Roman Emperor (Frederick Barbarossa), the king of France (Philip II) and the king of England (Richard I). Frederick died on the way and Philip returned to France. Richard defeated Saladin, but failed to recapture Jerusalem. Both leaders gained a reputation for bravery, and colourful legends were soon being told about them.

The crusading spirit was already dying. Most knights went on crusade now to make a fortune, not to fight for their religion. The Fourth Crusade (1204), instead of fighting the Muslims, took over Constantinople. There were many later crusades, and Louis IX of France had some successes in the 13th century. But by 1300 the whole region, except for a few coastal castles, was again in Muslim hands.

Above: *After his victory at Hattin (1187), Saladin captured Jerusalem. More merciful than the Crusaders, he allowed those inhabitants who wanted to leave to pass unharmed. In a later battle, when the English King Richard's horse was killed, Saladin sent him another, saying he did not like to see so great a warrior fighting on foot.*

*The crusade against the Muslims in Spain ended when the Muslim kingdom of Granada, ruled from the palace-fortress of the Alhambra, fell to the forces of Aragon and Castile in 1492.*

# The Later Middle Ages

Europe in about 1300 was still largely forest and swamp, and human society was still divided into those who fought, those who worked and those who prayed. Women were either housewives or nuns; few had other jobs. But society was changing. A growing number of people – merchants, bankers, skilled craftsmen – did not fit the old divisions. Town life was growing too, and in Western (but not Eastern) Europe, the feudal system was breaking down. Royal power was increasing, at least in some countries, and royal government was becoming more specialized.

*The most prosperous regions of Europe in the late Middle Ages were northern Italy and the Low Countries, where business and town life were most advanced.*

**Townsfolk and peasants**
Europe contained few cities of over 50,000 people, and townsfolk made up only a small (but growing) proportion of the population. Most towns were dominated by a small upper class of landowners or rich merchants. Craftsmen belonged to guilds, which controlled local business and looked after their own members.

In the country, serfdom was in decline. More and more landlords let out their land for rent, cash payments instead of services. Most armies were now made up of mercenaries, not ordinary men. The peasants, whether they were free men or serfs, were upset both by old grievances and new developments, and sometimes rose in rebellion against their lords.

In the 14th century these changes were complicated by a natural disaster, an epidemic of the disease of plague known as the Black Death, which helped to prevent populations growing. Falling population and fewer workers in turn caused higher wages, which meant higher prices and higher taxes – which in their turn caused more disturbances among the people.

## THE BLACK DEATH

The Black Death, which was an outbreak of the most infectious form of the disease called plague, started in Asia and swept through Europe from 1347 to 1350. About 30 per cent of the European population died, as well as many in Asia. Whole villages were wiped out. People did not understand the cause, and believed the plague was a punishment from God.

## Kingdoms and governments

Medieval Europeans had little idea of belonging to a 'state' or 'nation'. Kingdoms were the estates of kings, and might be increased by inheritance or war. To create strong royal government, kings had to enforce their authority on their vassals. The king of France had an especially hard job, because he controlled only a small territory and had some very powerful vassals, including the king of England. However, a larger and stronger kingdom was created in France by 1500, after a series of wars (known as the Hundred Years' War) against England, and in some other countries, including England and Spain. But Germany and Italy, for example, remained divided into small, more or less independent states.

Royal government meant simply the king and his chief courtiers, but from the 12th century special government departments began to develop. One example was the English Exchequer, named for the check tablecloth on which the officials counted out money. It became the custom for kings to

summon assemblies of local representatives. These assemblies were required to provide information which would make it easier to collect taxes, but we can see in them the beginnings of modern parliaments.

Above: *The Hanseatic League was an association of German merchant towns which gained monopolies – special agreements allowing no competitors – of much of the trade of northern Europe.*

Below: *Noblemen of the Middle Ages enjoyed falconry.*

# References

**Albigensians** A group of heretics in southern France, named after the city of Albi; a crusade was launched against them in 1209.

**Al-Idrisi** (1100–66) Arab scholar, author of a world geography containing 70 maps.

**Anglo-Saxon Chronicle** An account of Anglo-Saxon (English) history written in about 890.

**Arianism** A Christian heresy of the 4th to 7th centuries, holding that Jesus Christ was not God.

**Basil II** (reigned 976–1025) Byzantine emperor who waged constant war for 50 years, especially against the Bulgarians.

**Benedict of Nursia** (died about 547) Christian saint who founded the monastery of Monte Cassino, headquarters of the Benedictine order of monks.

**Carolingians** Dynasty of Frankish kings who ruled 751–987.

**Charles Martel** ('the Hammer', 689–741) Frankish leader (grandfather of Charlemagne) whose victory over a Muslim army near Poitiers (732) checked the Muslim advance into Western Europe.

**Christendom** Christian Europe.

**Convent** A community or 'house' for female members (nuns) of a religious order.

**Excommunication** Barring a person (or persons) from the Christian Church, a powerful weapon of medieval popes and bishops against political rulers.

**Franconia** Homeland of the Franks, central Germany.

**Frederick I** ('Barbarossa', reigned 1152–90) Holy Roman Emperor, greatest ruler of the German Hohenstauffen dynasty, drowned on the Third Crusade.

**Friars** Members of Christian religious orders, such as Franciscans and Augustinians, first founded in the 13th century, who, unlike monks, went about among the people, preaching, teaching and living on charity.

**Gothic** A word describing the culture, especially art, of the Middle Ages, about 1100–1500.

**Harun al-Rashid** (ruled 786–809) Caliph of Baghdad, greatest of the Abbasid caliphs, rich, clever and powerful, but who later lost authority in North Africa.

**Hejira** (Arabic 'flight') The flight of Muhammad from Mecca in 622, marking the first year of the Muslim calendar.

**Heraclius** (575–641) Byzantine general and (from 610) emperor, who saved the empire by defeating the Persians, but was later less successful against the first Muslim attacks.

**Heretics** People who rejected the official teaching of the Church, such as the Albigensians.

**Iconoclasm** The breaking of religious pictures, sculptures, etc; Iconoclasts caused a long crisis in the Byzantine empire, 726–842.

**Innocent III** (1161–1216) Pope (from 1198) who brought the papacy to the height of its power, able to dethrone an emperor.

**Inquisition** A department of the Church founded in 1232 to seek out heretics (the famous Spanish Inquisition was not founded until 1479 and was closely linked with the Spanish government).

**Investiture conflict** The quarrel between the Church and political rulers over who had the right to appoint (or 'invest') bishops and abbots.

**Lombards** A Germanic people settled in Italy, chief rival to papal power in Italy until defeated by Charlemagne.

**Louis IX** (1214–70) King of France (from 1226) known as Saint Louis, whose reign was long and fairly peaceful in spite of a six-year absence on crusade.

**Manzikert, Battle of** A victory of the Seljuk Turks over the Byzantines, which resulted in the conquest of Asia Minor by the Turks and the end of the old Byzantine army.

**Mecca** Holy Muslim city in Arabia, containing the Kaaba, a shrine that existed before Muhammad.

**Mercenaries** Soldiers who fight for anyone who pays them; in late medieval Europe most mercenaries were Swiss or German.

**Merovingians** Dynasty of Frankish kings who reigned 428–751.

**Middle Ages** The period of European history from the fall of the Roman empire to the Renaissance.

**Philip II** (1165–1223) King of France (from 1180) known as Philip Augustus, who greatly enlarged the French kingdom and made France a leading power.

**Pilgrims** People who make a journey to a holy place as an act of religious devotion, such as Muslim pilgrims to Mecca, English Christians to Canterbury, etc.

**Richard I** ('the Lionheart', 1157–99) King of England (from 1189), a famous warrior who spent most of his reign on crusade and as a prisoner.

**Roger II** (1095–1154) Norman ruler of Sicily, who succeeded his father, Roger I, and increased his lands by conquering Byzantine possessions.

**Sagas** Heroic stories written in Iceland in the 12th to 14th centuries, some being pure legend, others based on facts.

**Seljuk Turks** Turkish ruling dynasties of the 11th to 13th centuries; under Alp Arslan, they took Asia Minor from the Byzantines.

**Serfs** Peasants who were tied to the land by the rights over them held by their landlord; though not free, they were not slaves, as the landlord did not own them.

**Vassal** A tenant in the feudal system, who owed certain duties to his landlord, especially the duty to fight for him.

**Vinland** ('Wineland') A part of North America discovered by Norsemen from Greenland; no one knows exactly where it was.

# *The Birth of Modern Europe*

# The Renaissance

The Renaissance is the name given to the period that marks the end of the Middle Ages in Europe and the beginning of 'modern' history. The name means 'rebirth', and refers to the revival of interest in Classical (Greek and Roman) art, literature and ideas which began in 15th century Italy. Through studying the Classics, people came to think more deeply about their own times. In particular, they became more interested in the mind and body of human beings and the world in which we live. Since Classical civilization had existed before the Christian Church, many people ceased to believe that the Church had the answer to every question.

*Nikolaus Copernicus.*

## Italian art

The small, rich city-states of northern Italy, such as Florence and Venice, were the leaders of European civilization. They had created the first banks and capitalist business companies. Their leaders were not only landowning nobles but also merchants and bankers. Such powerful men wanted their cities to look splendid, with fine churches, palaces and public buildings. They had the money to pay for beautiful buildings and works of art, and they found artists to do the work. Why Florence, for example, should have produced so many fine artists is a mystery. But just as good generals come forward in wartime, great artists, perhaps, are found when they are needed.

The ideas of the Italian Renaissance spread steadily, first to France, and eventually throughout Europe. Northern Europe, especially the cities of Germany and the Low Countries, were centres of learning and experiment. The greatest scholar of the age was a Dutchman, Erasmus. The new art of oil painting developed in the Netherlands. Printing, which enabled ideas to spread much faster, was invented in Germany.

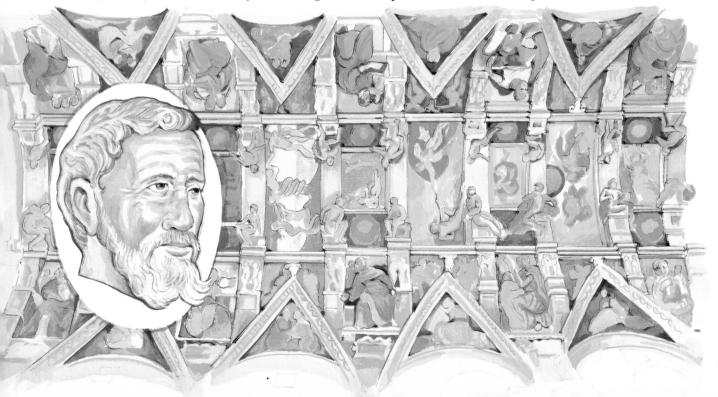

*Michelangelo (inset) and the Sistine Chapel ceiling.*

## Renaissance governments

In Renaissance Europe new forces were at work, forces which were not yet fully understood. One was capitalism – the use of money to create business and profits. Another was nationalism. Strong royal governments like those of France or England appealed to their subjects as 'Frenchmen' and 'Englishmen', especially when they wanted them as soldiers. However, the aims of governments did not change greatly. Dynastic rulers were still eager to increase their lands and their power, by marriage or by war.

Machiavelli's book, *The Prince*, shocked some people by saying that the chief aim of a ruler was to make his rule secure, not to rule well or kindly. However, that had always been the aim of governments, and it still is, though they do not admit it.

The main dynastic struggle in the early 16th century was between the House of Valois (kings of France) and the House of Habsburg (Holy Roman Emperors and kings of Spain). European conflicts contained one new ingredient after 1517 – a division in the Christian Church.

### RENAISSANCE SCHOLARS

Renaissance scholars were interested in everything, and were no longer restricted by the teaching of the Church. Nikolaus Copernicus (1473–1543), a Polish-born priest, proved that the Earth circles the Sun. His work was banned by the pope because it contradicted official Church teaching.

Science made many other advances. Andreas Vesalius (1514-64) dissected human bodies to find out about human anatomy. So did Leonardo da Vinci (1452–1519), though for a different reason – he was an artist, not a physician. Leonardo also drew plans of marvellous machines, including what look like a helicopter and a submarine, though they were never built, and would not have worked.

Michelangelo (1475–1564) was perhaps the greatest of Renaissance artists. Although a sculptor first and foremost, his largest finished work was a religious painting that covers the ceiling of the Sistine Chapel in the Vatican in Rome.

### JOHANN GUTENBERG

Johann Gutenberg (died 1468) worked in his printing shop in Mainz, Germany. He produced the first book (a copy of the Bible) to be printed with movable metal type.

Left: *In England, Renaissance culture reached its peak in literature. The plays of William Shakespeare (1564–1616), were performed in public theatres.*

# Discovery

Medieval Europeans knew little of the world. Some still thought the Earth was flat, and that if they sailed too far they would fall off the edge. Others believed that if they sailed too far south they would be burned black. Few ships sailed far out of sight of land. Other people had made long voyages before. The Polynesians, for instance, had sailed thousands of miles across the unknown Pacific Ocean to settle on islands as far apart as Hawaii and New Zealand. The Chinese traded with East Africa in the early 15th century. About that time, European ships began to sail on voyages of discovery. Within 100 years, they had crossed all the oceans and reached all the continents (except Australasia and Antarctica). The main reason for these exploring voyages was the desire to find a direct trade route from Europe to the Far East.

## The Spaniards

Meanwhile Christopher Columbus had gained the powerful support of Spain for his plan to reach the East by sailing west. In 1492 he crossed the Atlantic and reached some islands which he thought were the (East) Indies. They were, in fact, the West Indies. The Spaniards soon moved on to the American mainland. They conquered the two chief American civilizations, the Aztecs in Mexico and the Incas in Peru. With great cruelty and violence, they created a huge, all-powerful Spanish empire in the New World of America.

In 1494, the Portuguese and the Spaniards agreed to divide the world between them. Spain took the west, Portugal the east, and no trespassing was allowed. However, this agreement did not last long. Other nations began to take an interest in the New World. The French and English sailed to North America, and eventually founded their own colonies there. By the 17th century they had trading companies in India too, while another great sea power, the Dutch, were taking over from the Portuguese in the Far East.

## The Portuguese

Portugal was a small, poor country, but it lay on the corner of Europe, in the best position for Atlantic voyages. In the 15th century Portuguese ships set off southward along the coast of Africa. They hoped to find a way through to the east and also to find an ally against the Muslims in the legendary Christian ruler, Prester John, who was supposed to reign somewhere 'in the East'. Year by year the ships sailed cautiously farther and farther south, until Bartolomeu Dias rounded the Cape of Good Hope (South Africa) in 1488. In 1497–98 Vasco da Gama sailed north, along the East African coast. To his surprise he discovered a Muslim civilization in cities like Mozambique and Mombasa. Guided by an Arab pilot, he reached India. Other voyagers followed him, winning control of Indian Ocean trade from Arab, Persian and Indian merchants. The Portuguese advanced to Indonesia and, eventually, to China and Japan.

*Europeans were eager for new trade, and they were ready to use force to gain it.*

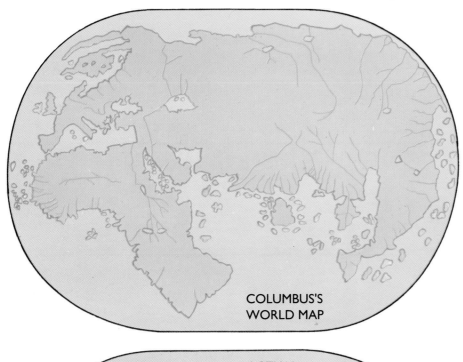

COLUMBUS'S
WORLD MAP

ACTUAL
WORLD MAP

## VOYAGES OF DISCOVERY

Columbus believed that the Earth was smaller than it is and that the Asian continent stretched much farther east. When he accidentally discovered America, it lay roughly where he had expected to find Asia, so it is not surprising that he thought he was near Japan and China.

The ships in which Europeans discovered the oceans were the product of two shipbuilding traditions: the tough, stubby, square-sailed vessels of northern Europe; and the slimmer, nimbler craft of the Mediterranean.

Muslim merchants in India resented the Portuguese arrival. But the Portuguese were determined, and they had greater firepower.

| | |
|---|---|
| 1488 | Dias (Portugal) rounds Cape of Good Hope |
| 1492 | Columbus (Spain) discovers West Indies |
| 1497 | John Cabot (England) discovers Newfoundland |
| 1498 | Vasco da Gama (Portugal) reaches India |
| 1519–22 | Magellan's ship (Spanish) sails around the world |
| 1534 | Jacques Cartier (France) discovers the St Lawrence River (Canada) |

*Above left: Columbus's world map, and the world as we know it.*
*Below: Columbus's ships.*

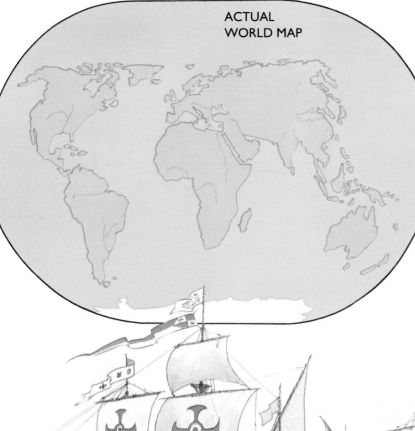

# Reformation

The breakdown of feudalism was one sign that medieval civilization was coming to an end in Europe. Another was the unpopularity of the Church. People were no less religious. They were not unhappy with Christianity, only with the rulers of the Church, from the Pope down. The Church needed to be reformed. But, as often happens in history, what started as a movement for reform turned into a revolution. The protesters founded separate Churches which did not recognize the authority of the Pope and taught different beliefs. Europe became divided into Roman Catholics (loyal to the old Church headed by the Pope) and Protestants, who belonged to new, reformed Churches. Though still Christian, in effect they represented a new religion.

## Papal power

The popes of the Renaissance spent more time increasing their own power and wealth than acting as spiritual leaders. They had built up the Papal States into one of the largest territories in Italy, and ordinary people saw them as no different from other power-hungry Italian princes. Bishops too were often greedy and ambitious men who lived a life of luxury and seldom visited the churches for which they were responsible. Some parish priests were ignorant louts; some monks behaved no better than criminals, treating their sacred vows as a joke.

One example of the rot that had set in was the sale of Indulgences. These were bits of paper which carried a promise of forgiveness of sins to anyone who bought them: 'Give us your money and you'll go to heaven!'

## Luther

The selling of Indulgences was one of the corrupt practices attacked by Martin Luther, a German monk and teacher of theology at Wittenberg, in 1517. Luther did not believe that sinners could be saved by buying scraps of paper. He believed that sinners were forgiven through the power of God's love, and this could only be gained by the sinner's personal faith in God.

Luther wanted the Church to change its ways. The reaction of the Pope was to excommunicate him (expel him from the Church). Luther's friends came to his support, and his criticism of the Church became stronger. In a famous debate at the Diet (assembly) of Worms (1521), Luther defended his beliefs. When he refused to back down, agreement became impossible: the division between Church and protesters was permanent.

*Luther defends his views at the Diet of the Holy Roman Empire, presided over by the Emperor Charles V.*

## The Reformation spreads

Politics and religion were interlinked in the 16th century, and many people supported Luther for political reasons. Once rid of the Pope's authority in his realm, a Protestant ruler also gained control of valuable Church lands. King Henry VIII of England rejected Rome mainly because the Pope refused to allow him to divorce his wife.

The Protestants, as Luther's followers were called, were divided among themselves. Other reformers set up their own Churches. Huldrych Zwingli in Zurich told his congregation that only God's chosen people (themselves) would be 'saved'. John Calvin, in Geneva, preached an even stricter form of Christianity, and his influence spread more widely than Luther's. Fighting broke out in Germany between a League of Protestant princes and the Catholic forces of the Holy Roman Emperor, Charles V. The quarrel was patched up at the Diet of Augsburg (1555). There it was agreed that the religion of any German state should be decided by its ruler. But this agreement did not prevent future religious wars.

Above: *The French reformer, John Calvin (1509–64), preaching in Geneva. His Institutes of the Christian Religion (1536) gave Protestantism a clear theology, which Lutheranism lacked.*

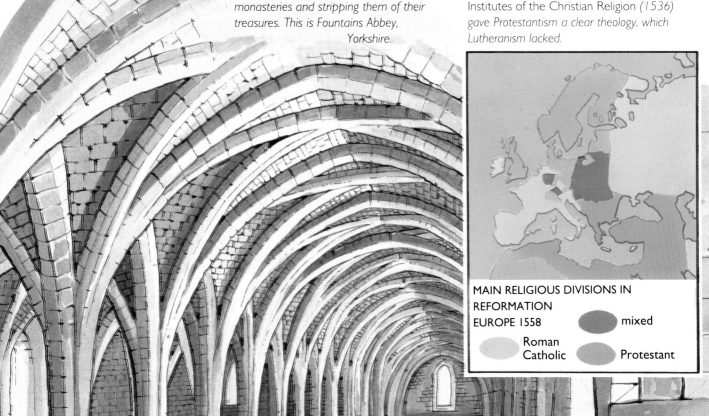

*In England, King Henry VIII gained vast Church estates by closing down all monasteries and stripping them of their treasures. This is Fountains Abbey, Yorkshire.*

MAIN RELIGIOUS DIVISIONS IN REFORMATION EUROPE 1558

mixed

Roman Catholic

Protestant

# Religious Wars

Religious differences increased the divisions and hatred between people. The Roman Church fought back against Protestantism in a campaign known as the Counter-Reformation, in which a new religious order, the Jesuits, played an important part. France was torn by a bloody civil war between Protestants and Catholics. The Protestant Dutch fought all the more fiercely for independence from Catholic Spain. Spain and England became bitter enemies, and most European states were engaged in the conflict known as the Thirty Years' War.

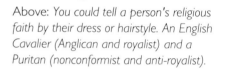

## French wars

France remained officially Catholic, but contained a large number of Protestants, known as Huguenots. A series of savage civil wars were fought between the two groups. In 1589 a Huguenot prince, Henry of Navarre, inherited the crown. He became a Catholic to gain acceptance, but by the Edict of Nantes (1598) he made the Huguenot faith legal.

## The Netherlands

One of the most prosperous countries in Europe, the Netherlands were ruled by Spain. Inspired by William the Silent, Prince of Orange, Holland and other northern provinces of the Netherlands declared their independence in 1579. In spite of many defeats – and the murder of William in 1584 – the Dutch fought on until Spain was forced to sign a truce in 1609. The United Provinces became an independent republic.

The Dutch received some help from Protestant England.

That was one reason why Philip II of Spain sent an armada, or invasion fleet, against England in 1588. Helped by strong winds, the English drove off the armada, with the loss of many Spanish ships.

*Above: You could tell a person's religious faith by their dress or hairstyle. An English Cavalier (Anglican and royalist) and a Puritan (nonconformist and anti-royalist).*

*Below: In 1572, during a truce in the French Religious Wars, Catholic leaders plotted to kill the chief Huguenots, who were in Paris to attend a wedding, on St Bartholomew's Day (24 August). The plot to murder one or two men turned into a massacre, in which thousands of Huguenots died.*

## ENGLISH CIVIL WAR

Religious quarrels played a part in the English Civil War (1642–46), a struggle for power between king and parliament. Parliament won, with Scottish help, and King Charles I was beheaded (1649). The victorious Parliamentary general, Oliver Cromwell, had become Lord Protector, king in all but name, by his death in 1658. Failure to find a successful form of republican government resulted in the recall of the executed king's son as Charles II in 1660.

*Oliver Cromwell.*

*The Thirty Years' War began with a Protestant–Catholic quarrel in Bohemia (Czechoslovakia). In one incident (the 'Defenestration of Prague') two Catholic imperial council members were thrown out of the window of Prague castle. They landed in the moat and were not badly hurt.*

## The Thirty Years' War

This conflict was really a series of wars between 1618 and 1648. It began as a civil war among the states of Germany, between the Protestant princes and their overlord, the Holy Roman Emperor. Spain and Austria, like the Empire, were under Habsburg rule and helped the Catholics. This drew in Protestant powers on the other side. The most remarkable general was the Protestant king, Gustavus Adolphus of Sweden, who won striking victories against Habsburg forces.

Later in the war, France joined Sweden. Though France was a Catholic power, she was also the chief rival and old enemy of the Habsburgs. The entry of France on the side of the Protestants showed that religion was no longer the chief motive for war. The French strategy eventually proved successful, for by the time of the Treaty of Westphalia (1648), it was clear that the mighty Habsburg power was shrinking. The most powerful force in Europe was France.

In spite of war, Europe grew richer in the 17th century. Its population was rising as a result of more productive farming. Trade was increasing, thanks to banks and capitalist business methods such as joint-stock companies. Industry was still a matter of small workshops, not factories, but mining and engineering expanded to meet the needs of war. In Eastern Europe, change was slower. There, feudalism continued, and landowning nobles dominated the mass of peasant farmers.

# References

**Anglicanism**   The religion of the Church of England, closer to Roman Catholicism than other Protestant Churches, both in its worship and its organization.

**Cabot, John** (1450–98)   Italian navigator in English service, who discovered North America in 1497, making a second voyage in 1498.

**Charles V** (1500–58)   Holy Roman Emperor (1519–56) and King of Spain (1516–56), who was the chief defender of Catholicism in the Reformation; his personal possessions (including Spanish America) were enormous but they were not united as one empire.

**Columbus, Christopher** (1446–1506) Italian navigator in Spanish service, who discovered America in 1492 and made three more voyages to the Caribbean.

**Counter-Reformation**   The reform movement in the Roman Catholic Church which fought back against Protestantism and, at the Council of Trent (1545–63), raised standards among the clergy and tightened up Church discipline; other 'weapons' of the Counter-Reformation included the Jesuits and the Spanish Inquisition.

**Da Gama, Vasco** (1469–1524) Portuguese commander of the first expedition to India (1497–98), a good leader but a poor diplomat who relied on force and bluster.

**Diet**   The name of the assembly of ruling princes and representatives of the chief towns in Germany, presided over by the Holy Roman Emperor.

**Erasmus, Desiderius** (1466–1536) Dutch scholar and teacher, a supporter of religious reform but not of the Protestant Reformation, the greatest figure of the renaissance of learning in northern Europe.

**Habsburgs**   German royal dynasty who became rulers of Germany and the Holy Roman Empire, of Spain, and other countries; they ruled in Austria until 1918.

**Humanism**   A word that describes the general philosophy of Renaissance thinkers (like Erasmus), descended from Classical Greece, in which the greatest value is placed on the ideas and achievements of human society; such thinking undermined the authority of the Church, which regarded the activities of human beings on Earth as unimportant.

**Jesuits**   Members of the Society of Jesus, a religious order founded by Ignatius Loyola in Spain in 1540; Jesuits were active in the Counter-Reformation and acted as missionaries to non-Christians as far away as Japan.

**Joint-stock company**   A business association, which raises money by selling stock or shares in the company; trading expeditions were often financed in this way.

**Low Countries**   The region which is now Belgium, the Netherlands and Luxembourg.

**Machiavelli, Niccolo** (1469–1527) Florentine official, author of a book on government, *The Prince*; our word 'Machiavellian' means devious and sinister, but Machiavelli's work was not wicked so much as free-thinking and practical.

**Magellan, Ferdinand** (1480–1521) Portuguese navigator in Spanish service who led the expedition that reached the Moluccas by sailing west around Cape Horn in 1521; one of his ships sailed on around the world.

**Peasants' Revolt** (1524)   A rebellion in Germany of townspeople and peasants against laws, taxes and landlords, partly inspired by the Lutheran Reformation; the rebels were easily and savagely crushed by soldiers.

**Philip II** (1527–98)   King of Spain (from 1556), the most powerful Catholic ruler in Europe, yet unable to put down the rebellion in the Netherlands or to invade England as he planned in 1588.

**Presbyterianism**   A form of Protestantism in which the Church is governed by 'elders', based largely on Calvin's teaching; it became especially strong in Scotland.

**Prester John**   A legendary Christian ruler whose kingdom was believed to lie somewhere in the East; the legend may have grown from rumours about Ethiopia, where Christianity had been introduced in the 4th century.

**Puritans**   A name given to those people in England who wanted a 'pure' Church, like the early Christian Church, and considered the Church of England was too much like Roman Catholicism.

**Reformation**   The religious revolution in 16th century Europe which destroyed the unity of the medieval Christian Church and resulted in the creation of separate, Protestant Churches.

**Renaissance** ('rebirth')   The changing ideas about learning and the arts in Europe about 1400–1600, which included the revival or rediscovery of Classical culture, the questioning of religious belief, a more scientific approach to knowledge, and striking new developments in art and literature; it forms an interval between 'medieval' and 'modern', and was a period in which the pace of change speeded up.

**Tordesillas, Treaty of** (1494) An agreement between Spain and Portugal to divide the world between them for purposes of trade, Spain getting the western half and Portugal the east; the line drawn on the map through the Atlantic left Brazil (then unknown to Europe) to Portugal, which is why the Brazilians today speak Portuguese, not Spanish.

**United Provinces**   The name of the first independent Dutch state.

**Valois**   French royal dynasty which reigned from 1328 to 1589.

**Vatican**   The headquarters of the Pope in Rome.

# The Age
# of Absolutism

# France under Louis XIV

In 17th century Europe, as in other continents, a country's government was usually headed by a monarch. He held supreme power, at least in theory, and few people questioned that power. In the Middle Ages, royal power had been checked by the great landowning barons. By about 1500 European kings had enforced their authority over the landowners, and often employed paid officials to run the government instead of nobles with powers and ambitions of their own. There were other checks on royal power, such as the need to raise money through taxes. A government which put too much pressure on its subjects, through harsh taxation or other means, risked rebellion. Nevertheless, royal power was at its height in the 17th century, and nowhere more than in France.

## Louis XIV

Germany and Italy were still divided into small, independent states. The power of Spain, in spite of the silver and gold shipped from Spanish America, was fading. France had the biggest population, the most skilful craftsmen, fertile soil, good trading ports (on both the Mediterranean and the Atlantic) and the best army. During the long reign of Louis XIV (1643–1715), France was the leading power in Europe.

'I am the State', Louis is supposed to have said, and he governed France like a private estate. He lived in extraordinary luxury in the palace he had built at Versailles, surrounded by rich but unproductive aristocrats, and he had the last word in every argument, even in religion or art.

During the first half of the 17th century, the French government was controlled by two clever cardinals, Richelieu and Mazarin. From 1661, when Louis became old enough to rule, until 1683, he was served by able ministers. However, the whole system of government and economy in France was old-fashioned and unfair. Long before Louis's death, signs of weakness appeared.

Left: *King Louis XIV lived in the magnificence of Versailles, where it took twelve servants over an hour to light the candles in the Hall of Mirrors. The French king lived a life of public ceremony.*

NEWTON INVESTIGATING LIGHT

Science took giant strides in the 17th century as a result of changes in mental attitude. People no longer accepted what they were told by some authority (such as the Church). Following the teaching of René Descartes (1596–1650), many educated people believed in the power of human reason to discover the facts about the universe. There were many inventions and discoveries by scientists (especially mathematicians). Isaac Newton (1642–1727) investigated light and worked out the theory of gravity to explain how the universe works.

## Wars

France was engaged in a series of wars. They were caused partly by Louis's ambition and partly by fears of French power in other countries. The huge cost of these wars, in men and money, slowly wore France down. The last and greatest of them was the War of the Spanish Succession (1702–13). An alliance of France's enemies, led by England and the Netherlands, inflicted heavy defeats on the French armies, which until then had seemed unbeatable. At Louis's death, France was still the greatest state in Europe, and his successor, Louis XV, lived at Versailles in equal splendour. But the balance of power was changing. France's rivals, both old (England) and new (Brandenburg-Prussia) were growing, while the French government and economy were in even more urgent need of reform.

*Above: By the end of Louis XIV's reign, the lower classes were crushed by heavy taxation, yet it was not enough to meet the huge spending of the royal government. Population was falling. So were prices, which ruined the most important people in the kingdom – the producers. Farming was in decline, and bad harvests led to a serious famine in 1709.*

*Below: Trade was growing in 17th century Europe, but all forms of land transport were slow and expensive. Goods were moved by water whenever possible.*

# Safavid Persia

Around 1500, the Islamic world covered an area larger than the area of Christendom, the Christian world. But Muslims were no more united than Christians, and, like Christianity, Islam entered a time of crisis in the early 16th century. For centuries it had contained many different sects or religious groups, but the two main branches were (and are) Sunni and Shi'a. Muslim rulers generally belonged to the Sunnite branch, which was better suited to organized government and religion (in Islam, politics and religion cannot be separated).

### Shah Ismail

The first stage of the crisis in Islam began in 1502 when Ismail, a descendant of a Persian saint who lived about 1300, made himself shah of Persia (Iran), though many years passed before he controlled the whole country. Ismail, described by a European visitor as 'brave as a gamecock', was a member of an extremist Shi'ite sect, and his followers regarded him as the rightful ruler of all Islam. They believed that the sultan of the Ottoman Turks, Persia's neighbour and chief rival, had no right to his throne, and this resulted in a long series of wars between Persia and the Ottoman empire.

### Abbas the Great

The greatest ruler of the Safavid dynasty was Shah Abbas, who reigned from 1586 to 1628. As great rulers had to be, he was successful in war. However, he is remembered best for skill in government, encouragement of trade, and tolerance in religion. Although a devoted Shi'ite, he was even willing to entertain Christians, since they brought useful trade. Though he expelled the Portuguese from Persia, he welcomed the English and the Dutch, and allowed Christian missions to be founded. He helped the growth of trade and industry by building roads, bridges and caravanserai for travelling merchants, and he made Persia, with its mixed population of Turks, Arabs and other races, a great nation once again. For all his good qualities, he shared the cruelty of so many supreme rulers, and he was willing to kill members of his own family to protect his own security.

*The finest memorial to Shah Abbas was his new capital city, Isfahan, which he changed from a small provincial town into a place of glittering mosques and pavilions. It became the centre of eastern Muslim culture for nearly 200 years.*

*The military success of Shah Abbas was due to his reorganization of the army. He turned it into a body of professional soldiers, instead of a loose collection of tribal groups loyal to their own chiefs. He received some advice and assistance from an adventurous Englishman, Robert Sherley, especially with artillery, which was more advanced in Europe.*

*As part of his efforts to make Persia a great power once more, Shah Abbas put his people to work building better roads, bridges and caravanserai (inns).*

## PERSIAN DECORATIVE ARTS

In Safavid Persia, the decorative arts reached a peak of brilliance. Besides patterned silks, book production, leatherwork, coloured tiles and many other artistic crafts, the most famous was the production of carpets – beautiful patterns based on flowers and animals and produced on a simple, upright loom. Like all Oriental rugs and carpets, they were knotted, not woven, and some silk carpets were so fine that they contained over 150 knots per square centimetre.

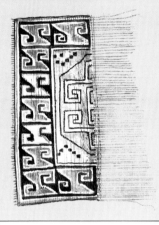

## Safavid decline

The successors of Shah Abbas were less able rulers, some of whom showed a talent only for murdering and massacring their opponents. Yet their subjects' respect for their dynasty was so great that the last Safavid did not disappear until 1736, when the throne was seized by Nadir Shah. He had begun his career as the leader of a gang of robbers, but proved to be a military genius. He drove out Russians, Turks and Afghans, who had seized Persian territory, and made Persia a bigger country than it had been under Shah Abbas. He was spoiled by success, growing cruel and greedy, and was murdered by his own bodyguard in 1747.

# The Ottoman Empire

The empire of the Ottoman Turks was the greatest power in the world in the 16th century. It reached into eastern Europe, and Europeans feared the whole continent might be overrun by the Turkish armies. The need to defend the Habsburg lands from the Turkish advance was one of the many tasks that occupied the Holy Roman Emperor, Charles V. Otherwise, he could have spent more time on German affairs and perhaps crushed the Lutheran Reformation.

*The janissaries were the core of the Ottoman army, trained from childhood and devoted to the sultan.*

### The rise of the Ottomans

The Ottomans took over when the Seljuk empire fell into ruins in the early 14th century. The early Ottoman sultans increased their territory (mainly at the expense of the Byzantine empire), until 1402, when they were suddenly halted by the invasions of the Mongols. This was only a brief setback. After the death of Timur (Tamerlane) in 1405, the Ottomans advanced again, capturing Constantinople in 1453 and finally ending the existence of the East Roman empire. For a time, the revival of Persia under the Safavids kept the Turks busy, but Selim the Grim (1512–20) crushed Shi'ite rebellion in his own lands and conquered Egypt and Syria, as well as part of Persia (eventually regained by Abbas the Great).

### Suleiman the Magnificent

Ottoman power reached its height under Selim's successor, Suleiman I (1520–66), whose court was so splendid that European visitors gave him the nickname 'the Magnificent'. (His own people, with different ideas about the duties of a ruler, called him 'the Lawgiver'.)

The keys to Ottoman success were the leadership of the sultan and the power of the

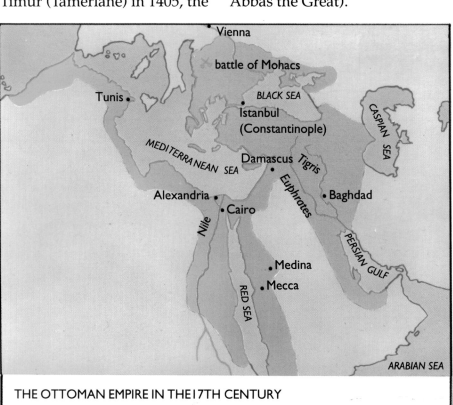

THE OTTOMAN EMPIRE IN THE 17TH CENTURY

*Suleiman the Magnificent.*

army, especially the skilled professional force known as the janissaries. In 1525, through his victory at Mohacs, Suleiman conquered Hungary. A few years later, his forces besieged Vienna, the capital of Habsburg Austria, though they did not capture it. In the east the Ottoman forces defeated the Persians. Their grip on the Mediterranean tightened when they took the island of Rhodes, as well as Aden and Algiers. Under Suleiman also, the Ottomans gained a navy, commanded by Khair-ed-din (called Barbarossa by Europeans), who operated from bases in North Africa. (By an agreement with France, the Turkish fleet was also able to spend the winter in the French port of Marseille.) However, the Turks were not a naval power by tradition, and they usually avoided battles with large

To assist in breaking down the walls of Constantinople, the Turks had a giant gun which, however, could be fired only once every three hours.

fleets. Their navy suffered a severe defeat at the battle of Lepanto in 1571, and never fully recovered.

## Decline of Ottoman power

The strength of the Ottoman empire depended largely on the sultan. Suleiman's successors were weaker men, too easily tempted by the soft life of the court. The Turkish economy was also weak. Although farming was productive, trade and industry were not. Capitalist methods, which proved so successful in encouraging economic growth in Europe, hardly existed.

Yet the Ottoman empire remained a great power for centuries. Under an energetic sultan or a clever grand vizier (chief minister), it sometimes prospered. In fact, it reached its largest extent in the late 17th century. But this was misleading. By 1800 the empire was on the point of collapse. It was kept going for another 122 years only by European powers who had their own reasons for propping it up.

The Knights of St John sail away from their headquarters on the island of Rhodes after its capture by the Turks in 1522.

# Mughal India

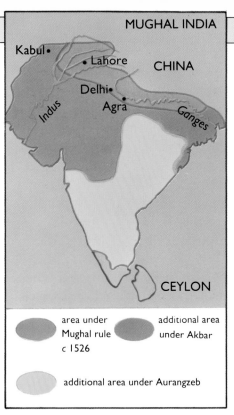

Another great Muslim empire was founded in the 16th century – in India. The Mughals, or Moghuls, were of Mongol origin, and they created the first strong central government in India since Tamerlane had captured Delhi in 1398. Although they won their empire by conquest, they maintained it by good government, until the 18th century when their power declined. Conquests and taxes made the Mughal court rich. Under the early emperors Mughal art, architecture and crafts, in which Indian and Persian styles were mixed, reached standards of extraordinary beauty.

## Akbar

The founder of the Mughal dynasty was Babur ('Tiger'), a princely Muslim warrior who had won his first battle at 14. By 1527 he made himself master of northern India, and although his successor, Humayan, was driven out of Delhi for a time, with Persian help he regained control.

The man who established Mughal rule firmly throughout most of India was Babur's grandson, Akbar, who reigned from 1556 to 1605. From 1560, when Akbar took over the government and army at the age of 17, he crushed rebellions and extended the empire deep into the Deccan. The princely warriors known as the Rajputs he defeated in war or won over by other means. He married the daughter of a Rajput, although she was a Hindu.

*Akbar hunting with cheetahs.*

Like Shah Abbas in Persia, Akbar felt strong enough to be tolerant, but his religious tolerance, very unusual for his time, was genuine. He attended Hindu festivals, listened to Jesuit missionaries, and tried to develop a new religion that included the best elements of all others. This experiment was not a success, but Akbar's rule was popular. He employed Hindus as local officials, and he brought peace and prosperity to people who had known neither. Complaints about his government came as often from Muslims as from Hindus. Akbar did not interfere much with Hindu customs, though he did try to stop the practice of *suttee* (forcing widows to commit suicide at their husbands' funerals by throwing themselves on the pyre).

Unlike his successors, Akbar was not highly educated, but he loved learning, literature and art.

The map legend reads:

- area under Mughal rule c 1526
- additional area under Akbar
- additional area under Aurangzeb

*Shah Jahan stands before the most famous of Mughal buildings, the lovely Taj Mahal, built as a memorial to his wife.*

## Successors of Akbar

Although Akbar's policy of tolerance was not abandoned, Mughal rule became harsher after 1605. Shah Jahan (reigned 1628–58) still employed Hindu officials, but ordered the destruction of Hindu temples (though the order was widely disobeyed). The activities of Christian missionaries caused trouble with both Hindus and Muslims, but on the whole Europeans had little effect on India until the 18th century. Then the Mughals' lack of a navy became a serious weakness, as European ships dominated the Indian Ocean and Bay of Bengal. Mughal power advanced farther and farther south, but at growing cost. Shah Jahan's great extravagance, and the cost of war, drained the government of money. Peasants fled to escape taxes, and the roads which Akbar had made safe were infested by bandits.

All these troubles came to a head in the reign of Aurangzeb (1658–1707). He held the empire together, but Mughal authority almost collapsed after his death. In 1738 Nadir Shah invaded, captured Delhi, killing thousands, and carried off the treasures of the Mughal court. There was no strong central power left in India, and the gap was filled by Europeans. By 1763 the greatest power in India was the British East India Company. The Mughal empire continued until 1858, when India came under British rule.

*English merchants at Bombay. Europeans were present in India from the time of Babur, but had little influence until the collapse of Mughal government in the 18th century.*

# Manchu China

The Ming dynasty in China lasted until the mid 17th century, although the later Ming emperors were so weak they sometimes controlled little more than their own palace. In the early 17th century the government allowed the tribal people of Manchuria, to the north, through the Great Wall to help fight rebels. They entered Pekin and in 1644 declared their own Manchu leader emperor. The Manchu were barbarians in the eyes of the Chinese, but they understood Chinese civilization and did not wish to harm it. In the course of the Manchus' long rule, China became a kind of living museum, where change was considered unnecessary and undesirable.

## Defence and conquest

The first task of the Manchu dynasty was to strengthen the frontiers in the north and north-west. As they advanced into Mongolia, the Chinese came into conflict with the Russians, who were expanding from the west. At this period, the Chinese were stronger, and Outer Mongolia became a Manchu province. The Manchu also conquered Tibet, though the Tibetans kept some independence, and extended Chinese authority over Korea, Indochina, Burma and Nepal.

The Manchu empire reached its greatest extent under Ch'ien-lung (1736–96). Like most multi-national empires, it provoked rebellions among minorities, such as the Muslim people of Kansu in the north. Financial problems caused more widespread discontent, and the Manchu emperor ordered the execution of authors who had written books that criticized the government. The refusal of the Manchu to consider making big changes, in spite of growing pressure from the West and demands for change from the peasants and the growing middle class, led to its downfall. The final breakdown was delayed until 1912, when the Manchu dynasty was swept away and China became a republic.

*Manchu tribesmen were allowed through China's defensive Great Wall by a Chinese general who wanted their help. After the Manchu had seized power in China, life continued much as before, though government officials were forced to wear 'pigtails' in the Manchu style.*

Although Chinese society was stiff and conservative, change was possible. For the European market, the Chinese learned to make pottery by new methods of mass production, and they invented new glazes and colours.

CHINESE CRAFTSMEN

The Emperor K'ang-hsi corrects the calligraphy (handwriting) in an official document. He was the greatest of the Manchu emperors and a learned man; the huge dictionary compiled in his reign is still used by historians of China. Chinese culture was mainly an upper-class concern. In China, the typical landowner or official was also an accomplished painter and poet. Professional craftsmen were not so highly valued as these skilled amateurs of the ruling class. Such artists aimed to produce work that was technically perfect, but not original. Because it was the product of a civilized person, it stuck to old traditions and Confucian respect for custom, discipline and delicacy.

## China and the West

In the first century of Manchu rule, China was peaceful and prosperous. Crops like maize and potatoes, introduced by Europeans, increased food production, and by the reign of K'ang-hsi (1661–1722) China had about 300 million people, making it by far the most populous country in the world.

In general, foreigners were unwelcome in China, but trade with the West became increasingly important. The main exports were pottery and tea, for which the Europeans usually paid in silver, as the Chinese had no desire for most European products. In the 19th century, the Europeans found a product they *could* sell to the Chinese, the drug opium. When the government tried to ban it, the British fought a war to force the Chinese to accept it.

Because Chinese agriculture was very productive, the population grew rapidly. By about 1800 it had grown too rapidly: food production could not keep up, and famine added to the problems of the Manchu emperors.

# Tokugawa Japan

Life in 16th century Japan was lively and varied – at least for the rich. What the country lacked was strong central government, which it gained under the rule of the Tokugawa shoguns (1615–1867). The Tokugawa imposed peace and security but at the cost of isolating Japan from the rest of the world. No foreigners were allowed in, no Japanese were allowed out. With the end of the shogunate and the restoration of the rule of the emperor, a great revolution occurred. From being a backward and largely feudal country, Japan became within a few years a strong, ambitious, modern state.

**The shogunate**

Unlike the Chinese, the Japanese in the 16th century welcomed foreign ideas. Jesuit missionaries made many converts, but the most important novelty brought in by Europeans was firearms.

In Europe, firearms had helped kings to create strong royal governments, because lesser lords could not afford guns. The same thing happened in Japan. The civil wars and general disorder ended with the creation of a strong central government by three men: the general Nobunaga (1534–82), who controlled most of Japan by the time of his murder; Hideyoshi (1537–98), who had once been Nobunaga's footman; and Tokugawa Ieyasu (1543–1616), who took the title of shogun and founded the Tokugawa shogunate.

Ieyasu and his successors persecuted Japanese Christians and forced out European merchants. They forbade travel, kept the daimyo (nobles) in order, and restricted the emperor to ceremonial duties only. Their aim was stability: everyone had his proper place in life and was expected to keep to it. The old ideals of honour, loyalty and austerity were upheld.

The system did not work perfectly. A large number of beggars and outcasts existed at the bottom of society. Peasants in the countryside died from famine, while the rich in the towns spent heavily on luxuries. Nor could the shoguns prevent all changes, such as the rise of the merchants – despised by the daimyo who nevertheless borrowed money from them.

However, Tokugawa Japan was one of the richest countries in the world, rich not only in resources and money,

*In Japan people were born into a certain class and were expected to remain in it. Hideyoshi grouped people into four main classes: samurai, farmer, craftsman and merchant.*

but in culture too. Besides such
thoroughly 'Japanese' arts as
traditional forms of theatre,
Japan developed new art forms
which were to have a strong
influence on other cultures,
especially the West. They
included colour-printed posters,
designed by the best artists, and
domestic architecture, using
plain wood, floor matting,
sliding panels and screens, as
well as garden design.

*The only Europeans who were allowed direct contact with Japan under the shogunate were Dutch merchants on the island of Deshima in Nagasaki harbour.*

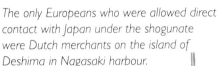

### The Meiji restoration

For nearly 700 years the
emperors had no real power.
When the Emperor Meiji
recovered his authority in 1867,
Japan began its rapid
development into a modern,
industrial state. This
revolution happened as the
result of the growing weakness
of the Tokugawa and pressure
from the United States, which
sent a naval force in 1854 to
force Japan to open its frontiers
to foreign trade. A new form of
government was created, and
industry and trade developed
fast. Japan built up an army
and navy powerful enough to
fight and win wars against
China (1894–95) and Russia
(1904–05).

*A daimyo on his way to court. The dress and ceremony were unchanged from centuries earlier. Economically too, the Japanese made little progress under the Tokugawa. When their isolation ended in the 19th century, they found they had been left behind. While the Japanese made the world's finest swords, other nations were making iron battleships. However, after 1867, the Japanese soon caught up.*

# The Rise of Russia

The victories of Gustavus Adolphus in the Thirty Years' War made Sweden the greatest power in northern Europe. Sweden produced another military genius in Charles XII (reigned 1682–1718), but his ambitious invasion of Russia in the Great Northern War ended in defeat. Russia was a backward country by European standards, but from 1682 to 1715 it was ruled by an energetic and determined tsar (emperor), Peter the Great, and made great progress. Although Russian society remained backward, the Russian empire became not only the chief power in the north but one of the great powers of Europe.

Russia arose from a group of Slav tribes united under the grand duke of Muscovy in the Middle Ages. They gained their religion and much of their culture from the Byzantine empire. Under tsars like Ivan the Terrible (reigned 1533–84), they increased their territory, mainly by conquest from the Tatar rulers in the south and east, but Russia remained largely cut off from Europe.

### 'Westernization'

Victory in the Great Northern War gave Peter the Great what he most desired: a port on the Baltic Sea to provide easier communications with Western Europe. He built a new capital, St Petersburg there, and hired European (especially French) experts to teach in the colleges and technical schools he founded and to advise on improvements in Russian industry, especially mining. Peter himself went to London to learn shipbuilding, to Germany to study gunnery and to Venice to study navigation. At home, he carried out sweeping reforms of Russia's medieval form of government. He destroyed the privileged and rebellious *streltsi*, originally created as the tsar's bodyguard. He abolished the class of boyars, the landowning aristocrats who had once ruled Russia with the tsar, and the old Duma, or council of state, and created a new civil service with officials appointed by himself. He increased Russian territory by war against Persia and Turkey, and sent expeditions to explore Siberia and discover Alaska.

The Russian tsar had great powers, greater even than those of Louis XIV of France. Peter terrified opponents by the force of his character (he beheaded rebels personally) and made full use of his powers. His successors were not all so capable, though Catherine the Great (reigned 1762–96) was no less formidable. Aided by her

The pioneers who led Russia's eastward expansion in Siberia were rough, warlike bands of Cossacks. Many of them were runaway serfs or army deserters. The government had no real control over them until the 18th century.

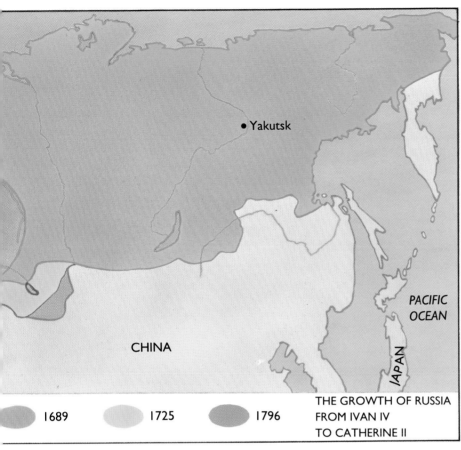

THE GROWTH OF RUSSIA
FROM IVAN IV
TO CATHERINE II

| | | |
|---|---|---|
| 1689 | 1725 | 1796 |

- Yakutsk

CHINA

JAPAN

PACIFIC
OCEAN

## Serfdom

The reforms of Peter changed nothing for the mass of the Russian population. More than half of them were serfs. They were unable to read or write and had few legal rights against the landowners for whom they worked. Thousands died through famine. The huge social problem of serfdom was left unsolved. In fact, under Catherine, the position of the serfs weakened. Rebellions of the peasants broke out more often. By 1800, a visitor to St Petersburg saw what looked like a modern, civilized society. But the modernity of Russia was only a thin layer, like a sheet of ice on a lake with dangerous currents below.

favourite and able minister, Gregori Potemkin, Catherine increased Russian territory without risking war with other European powers through, for example, the treaty of Kutchuk Kainardji and the Partition of Poland. Like Peter, she gave warm encouragement to the arts and science.

Below: *Peter the Great supervises the building of his magnificent new capital, St Petersburg (one of the most beautiful cities in Europe). He moved the government to St Petersburg from Moscow as a sign of his ambition to make Russia a 'Western' power. He employed German engineers and French architects for many projects, but he always appointed Russians, not foreigners, to posts in government.*

# References

**Alaska** The north-east peninsula of North America, 'discovered' by Bering for Russia in 1741 and sold to the United States in 1867.

**Aurangzeb** (1618–1707) Mughal emperor of India (from 1658), who seized the throne from his father, Shah Jahan, extended the frontiers by war but angered Hindu subjects by religious extremism.

**Bourbons** French royal dynasty which reigned 1589–1793, 1814–30 and (Bourbon-Orléans) 1830–48; other branches were kings of Spain (from 1700) and Naples (1735–1860).

**Boxer Rebellion** A nationalist rising against European influence in China in 1900 encouraged by the Manchu government but crushed by Western troops.

**Brandenburg** Medieval German state which merged with Prussia in 1618 and under Frederick William (reigned 1640–88) became a leading power in central Europe.

**Caravanserai** A type of inn, or 'caravan house', in the Middle East, usually built around a large courtyard, with accommodation for animals on the ground floor and people above.

**Dalai Lama** The name of the divine ruler and chief priest (lama) of Tibet, believed to be reincarnated (born again) in his successor.

**East India Company** The name of several European companies set up under government charters to trade in India and the Far East, of which the most important were the English (founded 1600) and the Dutch (1602); they became the means for European expansion and political power in Asia.

**Grand Vizier** The title of the chief minister of the Ottoman sultan.

**Great Northern War** A war (1700–09) caused by resentment of Swedish power, in which Charles XII of Sweden defeated Denmark, Poland, Saxony and Russia before invading Russia and suffering decisive defeat at Poltava (1709).

**Hong Kong** An island in south-east China which became a British trading base and, from 1841, a colony.

**India** A name that, until 1947, meant the whole peninsula of South Asia, including modern Pakistan, Bangladesh and Sri Lanka.

**Indochina** The south-east peninsula of Asia (including Thailand, Vietnam, Cambodia and Laos), which from ancient times contained various independent kingdoms; influenced by Hinduism and at times dominated by China.

**Ivan IV** ('the Terrible', 1530–84) Tsar of Russia (from 1533), a strong ruler but cruel and tyrannical, who greatly extended Russian territory in the south-east by victories against the Tatar khans.

**Kutchuk Kainardji, Treaty of** An agreement between Russia and Turkey in 1774 which gave Russia the right to 'protect' Orthodox Christians in Turkish-ruled south-east Europe, a perfect excuse for Russia to interfere in the Ottoman empire.

**Lepanto, Battle of** A naval battle in the Strait of Lepanto (Návpaktos), Greece, in 1571, when the Turkish fleet was destroyed by a Christian fleet including Venetian, Spanish and papal ships.

**Mahrattas** A Hindu people living mainly in the Western Ghats who formed a confederation and became a powerful force in 18th century India, when Mughal power was fading.

**Mazarin, Cardinal** (1602–61) Sicilian-born statesman who succeeded Richelieu as chief minister in France (1642) and, in spite of a short period in exile, ruled France and built up the basis of Louis XIV's power.

**Meiji** (1852–1912) Emperor of Japan (from 1867) who carried out many reforms. He abolished the old feudal system and encouraged Western ideas in business, education, law, etc.

**Opium War** A war fought by Britain against China in 1839–42 to force the Chinese to trade with the West, the immediate cause being Britain's wish to sell the drug opium to the Chinese.

**Ottoman empire** The Turkish empire founded and named after Osman about 1300 which held lands in Asia, Africa and Europe and survived until 1923.

**Poland** European kingdom whose king was elected (from 1572), a cause of weakness which led to the Partition, or division, of the country between Austria, Russia and Prussia in 1772–95.

**Rajputs** Indian knightly warriors who claimed descent from the Hindu warrior caste of *Kshatryas*; they lost their independence to the Mughals but continued their warrior traditions.

**Richelieu, Cardinal** (1585–1642) French statesman who became chief minister to Louis XIII in 1624 and was the effective ruler of France until his death.

**Safavids** The ruling Muslim dynasty in Persia, 1502–1736, the first truly Persian dynasty since the Sassanids.

**Spanish Succession, War of the** The last and greatest of the wars of Louis XIV, 1701–14, in which Austria, England and Holland tried to prevent Louis's grandson inheriting the Spanish crown; France suffered severe defeats but the Bourbon prince, Philip V, kept his crown.

**Sultan** The title of the ruler of a Muslim state, especially the ruler of the Turkish empire.

**Tatars** A people related to the Mongols who ruled much of Russia in the 14th century; their empire later broke up into independent *khanates* (kingdoms), gradually conquered by Russia.

**Tibet** A mountainous, Buddhist country between India and China, at times dominated, controlled and eventually (1950) seized by China.

# *Political Revolution*

# North American Colonies

North America did not offer Europeans easy riches like those the Spaniards found in Mexico, and no one rushed to settle there. The first colonies were founded in the 17th century, some by commercial companies, others by religious refugees (especially the English Puritans, who settled in parts of Massachusetts). The country proved productive, and by 1732 there were 13 English colonies along the east coast, from Maine to Georgia. French settlements existed to the north and west but, except in the St Lawrence valley, they were mostly trading posts, not permanent settlements.

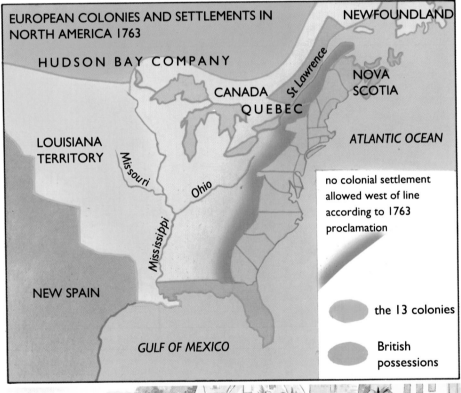

EUROPEAN COLONIES AND SETTLEMENTS IN NORTH AMERICA 1763

NEWFOUNDLAND

HUDSON BAY COMPANY

CANADA
QUEBEC
St Lawrence

NOVA SCOTIA

LOUISIANA TERRITORY

Missouri

Ohio

Mississippi

ATLANTIC OCEAN

no colonial settlement allowed west of line according to 1763 proclamation

the 13 colonies

British possessions

NEW SPAIN

GULF OF MEXICO

William Penn founded Pennsylvania in 1681. A Quaker devoted to good works, he did not cheat the local people, and the colonists lived in peace with them until 1755.

## Immigrants and natives

The native population of North America was thinly scattered, and that made it possible for European colonies to grow at their expense. To begin with, relations between the well-governed colonies of Massachusetts and their Algonkin neighbours were good. This was a misleading sign. In other parts, lawless European adventurers caused trouble. In spite of some cooperation between Europeans and native Americans, or 'Indians', by the 19th century the takeover of North America by people of European descent resulted in the almost complete destruction of the native American culture.

## The English colonies

These colonies, especially those in the north, developed their own customs without much interference from London. Most colonies had a royal governor and an elected assembly of representatives. By their control of taxation, the assemblies held some power in government. Some colonies were more democratic than Britain.

The colonies were not popular with the English government, partly because they contained many religious dissenters and partly because they did not play the part that colonies were expected to play. This was to supply the mother

An Algonkin village in Massachusetts in about 1700. The name Algonkin came from a group in the Ottawa region, but now includes a large number of different tribes and nations who speak (or spoke) the same basic language, and lived as far west as the Rocky Mountains. Algonkins, such as the Abnaki, Massachuset, Narraganset and Wampanoag, were the first native Americans met by European settlers. Although they were hunters and fishermen too, they were chiefly a farming people who lived in villages. They taught the first settlers some important lessons about farming in a new country – such as growing maize with fish as fertilizer.

country with cheap raw materials and to buy its manufactured goods in return. The southern colonies supplied Britain with rice, tobacco and other agricultural products, but the New England colonies provided little and formed their own manufacturing industries, such as shipbuilding.

The colonies grew rapidly in the 18th century, with new arrivals from other European countries. People of English descent were still the majority, but a growing number were native-born Americans. Cities like Philadelphia, Boston and New York (originally founded by Dutch settlers) were as large as European cities.

In 1763, after the Seven Years' War, the British government began to take a closer interest in North America. There were disagreements with the Americans. With France no longer a threat, colonists wished to go west, beyond the Allegheny Mountains, but the British government, fearing conflict with the Amerindians, prevented them.

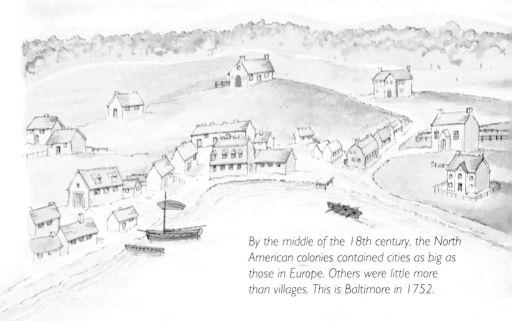

By the middle of the 18th century, the North American colonies contained cities as big as those in Europe. Others were little more than villages. This is Baltimore in 1752.

# The Spanish Empire

The largest American empire, stretching from California to Chile, belonged to Spain. Most of this huge territory was unsettled by Europeans, but by 1750 Mexico City was already larger than any European city except London and Paris. The Spanish colonies prospered in the 18th century, when economic reforms lifted the restrictions on trade, but the weakness of Spain itself and the example of successful revolutions in North America and France resulted in nationalist rebellions in the Spanish empire during the early 19th century. They led to the foundation of independent republics.

NORTH AMERICA

SOUTH AMERICA

under Spanish control

under Portuguese control

SPANISH AMERICA c 1600

## Immigrants and natives

European settlement had disastrous effects on the native population. The Arawaks, who were the first people met by Columbus and his followers, were wiped out completely by European diseases and through being forced to work for the Spaniards. During the first century of colonial rule, the native population in Spanish America fell sharply. Because the local people suffered and died when forced into hard labour, the colonists imported large numbers of Africans, captured and sold as slaves, to work their plantations and mines.

The colonial population, however, grew larger and richer during the 18th century, as the rigid rules which Spain attempted to enforce on its colonies were removed (partly because Spain could not enforce them). A cultured upper class developed, which kept in close touch with the latest fashions from Spain. But it did not affect the mass of native peasant society. The only part of Spanish culture they shared was religion. The Roman Catholic Church, with the Jesuits as its spearhead, was very powerful and sometimes acted like a branch of the government. The Church

spread European ideas – not only religious ones – and regarded itself as the protector of the native population. However, the Church was a conservative institution. To people who wanted a reform of society, especially those known as Creoles, it was the chief obstacle in the way of progress.

*African slaves endured great hardship working in the plantations and mines.*

## BRAZIL

The Portuguese colony of Brazil was a huge, largely unexplored territory. Until the 18th century, the chief colonial product was sugar, produced by a few wealthy plantations in the north-east. The discovery of gold, and later diamonds, brought rapid changes. Towns sprang up like mushrooms in the forest and fortune-hunters brought disease and death to the inhabitants. This is still happening now.

A Spanish colonial town in Mexico. Colonial society was deeply divided. Three races existed: the original native Amerindians (about half the total population), black Africans and people of European descent, plus many of mixed race. The top positions in government and society were held by Spaniards. The larger number of Creoles (people of mainly Spanish descent but Mexican-born) were kept out of these positions. These people, who were often rich and well-educated although under-privileged, became the leaders of movements for reform and independence.

**From silver to sugar**

The great power of Spain in the 16th century rested on silver from Mexican and South American mines. Without it, the expensive wars fought by Charles V and Philip II could not have been fought.

By the 18th century, other American products had become more important. Some of the Caribbean islands especially proved to be very fertile. They supplied Europe with sugar, tobacco and coffee. Sugar, which was unknown in medieval Europe, was an extremely profitable crop. Grown by slaves who did not have to be paid wages, it made huge fortunes for owners of plantations (some of whom did not even live in the New World).

At the treaty that ended the Seven Years' War in 1763, Britain was offered a choice of French possessions: Canada or the tiny, sugar-growing island of Guadeloupe. The British government chose Canada, to safeguard its North American colonies, but admitted that Guadeloupe was more valuable!

Simon Bolivar (1783–1830), the South American revolutionary hero. His inspiring leadership gained independence for Colombia, Venezuela, Ecuador and Peru.

# Trade, Colonies and War

During the 18th century European states fought a series of wars in the constant struggle to increase or maintain their territory. Alliances often changed, but Britain was always opposed to France, and Austria to Prussia. The British–French contest was worldwide, and the goal for which they fought was dominance of world trade. By 1763 Britain appeared to have won this contest. The French had been forced out of India and North America, but in America the British triumph was short-lived.

Below: *18th century warships were slow-moving wooden gun platforms carrying about 20 separate sails. The usual number of guns was 74 (some had more). An iron ball fired by one of these guns could smash through 1 metre (3 ft) of solid timber at a range of over 400 metres. The guns could fire other types of shot, such as grape (small iron balls in a canvas bag) and chain (iron balls linked by a chain), which ripped through the rigging of an enemy ship.*

## European rivalries

In the 18th century the most important political question in Europe was who would dominate Germany: the old Habsburg power based in Austria, or the new and rising power of Prussia? Frederick the Great of Prussia seized the rich Austrian province of Silesia, provoking the War of the Austrian Succession, 1740–48, in which Austria failed to regain its lost province. Yet Austria looked stronger. The shrinking power of the Ottoman empire removed a threat from the east: the Austrian Habsburgs regained Hungary from the Turks in 1699. However, the decline of the Turks was balanced by the rise of Russia. When Poland was partitioned (divided), Russia took the largest share, and it was Russia which, by changing sides in 1762 during the Seven Years' War, saved Prussia from almost certain defeat by Austria and its allies.

Above: *The activities of European nations brought people of many different races under their influence or control.*

## Trade and sea power

The struggle for trade and colonies was carried on by the seagoing nations – Spain and Portugal (the pioneers of overseas expansion), the Netherlands, France and Britain. The power of Spain and Portugal had faded, and although they still held territories overseas, they were not to be important colonial powers. It was the Dutch who first decided that trade was worth fighting for, and they took over most of the Portuguese trading posts in the East Indies, the Caribbean and West Africa. They also established a supply base for the Dutch East India Company in South Africa, which grew into a prosperous colony.

The activities of the Dutch brought them into conflict with the English. After three naval wars (1652–75) the English, who could easily block the English Channel – the Dutch 'highway' to the oceans – came out on top. That left England and France as the chief rivals for overseas trade. England, or Britain as it became after the Act of Union with Scotland in 1707, had one huge advantage. Britain was an island. It was not a great continental power, like France, and it played little part in the land campaigns on the continent, except to support its allies, who did the fighting, with money.

In the Seven Years' War (1756–63), the British gained great successes in India and North America, and the Peace of Paris which ended the fighting established Britain as the greatest sea power. France had suffered a setback, but not a disaster. She was soon to experience a greater crisis, which would change not only France, or Europe, but the world.

*West Indies trade made British merchants so rich and powerful in the 18th century that, as a group, they were able to influence government policy. One merchant started his career by sailing to Jamaica with a crate of tools, which he exchanged for sugar to sell back in England. Within a few years he was a rich man.*

# Africa and the Slave Trade

In the 18th century, the African 'product' most desired by European traders was neither pepper nor gold, but people. The trade in slaves from West Africa was very profitable. Although there were always some people who attacked this evil business, the slave trade continued for about 400 years, and left long-lasting wounds in relations between Europeans and Africans.

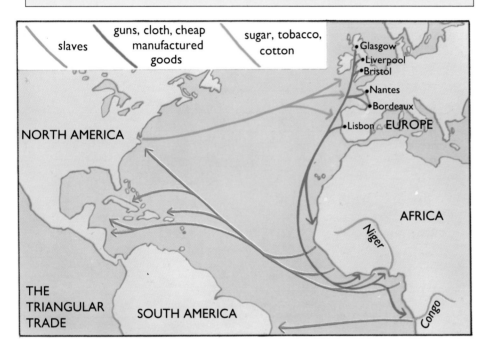

guns, cloth, cheap manufactured goods

slaves

sugar, tobacco, cotton

• Glasgow
• Liverpool
• Bristol
• Nantes
• Bordeaux
• Lisbon  EUROPE

NORTH AMERICA

AFRICA

Niger

THE TRIANGULAR TRADE

SOUTH AMERICA

Congo

## The slave trade

In the Sahel, the region south of the Sahara, several large Islamic empires rose and fell in the Middle Ages. They had contacts with North Africa, but little was known of them in Europe. When the Portuguese, followed by other Europeans, arrived in West Africa, no strong African power existed to prevent them building 'factories', or fortified posts, on the coast. These outposts became the centres for the supply of slaves. The slaves were sold in the American colonies, where cheap labour was wanted. Sugar, in particular, was grown on plantations that needed many workers.

Below: *Parts of southern Africa were beautiful and fertile, but guns and the slave trade destroyed thousands of villages between the 15th and 19th centuries.*

## The triangular trade

Europeans began trading in West African slaves as early as 1434, and by 1700 the trade had become big business. The right to supply slaves to the Spanish colonies in America was a treasured prize won by the British in the Peace of Paris (1713). Slave trading made the fortunes of many 'respectable' families. It changed Liverpool from a small port into a rich British city.

The transport of slaves in dreadful conditions from West Africa to the plantations of the Americas was one leg of a 'triangular' trade. The traders sold cheap manufactured goods (especially guns) to the Africans, carried slaves to the American colonies, and brought back American goods like sugar and tobacco to Europe. All three transactions earned large profits, barring accidents like shipwreck or the death of the slaves on the dreadful 'Middle Passage' across the Atlantic. By the time the trade was brought to an end in the early 19th century, about 20 million people had been carried into a life of slavery and hardship.

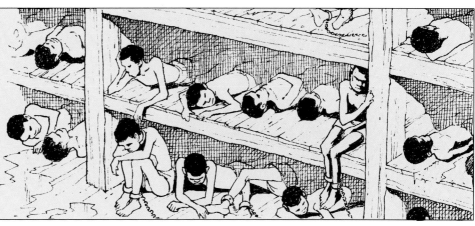

## SLAVERY

Slaves were packed into the hold of a slave ship like sardines in a can. Each person had just enough room to lie down. When they arrived in the West Indies, Virginia or Brazil, they were sold at auction. No effort was made to keep families together, and although not *all* slaves were badly treated by their owners, they had no chance of seeing their homeland or family again.

Above: A mosque in northern Nigeria. Islam spread from the north deep into Africa in the centuries after the Arab conquests. Except in a few places, Christian missionaries were not very active in Africa until the 19th century.

## East and South Africa

Slavery had always existed in Africa, as it had in other continents, although on a much smaller and less cruel scale. In East Africa the trade was mainly organized by Arabs, who supplied slave markets in the Middle East.

The East African coastal region possessed an ancient Swahili culture, a mixture of Arab and African tradition. But the once powerful African kingdoms inland, which had supplied the goods traded by the coastal states, had collapsed by 1600.

Africa contained only one large European settlement before the 19th century, the Dutch Cape Colony. Thanks to good farming land and the determination of the Dutch colonists, or Boers ('farmers'), the colony prospered. But as it expanded, it came into conflict with Bantu peoples, especially the warlike Zulu, and with Britain, which took over the Cape Colony in 1814. British authority in South Africa was confirmed by the Boer War (1899–1902) and the creation of the Union of South Africa (1910).

# Australia and New Zealand

Although Portuguese and Dutch sailors had touched on the western coasts of Australia and New Zealand in the 17th century, it was not until after 1763 that Europeans, chiefly British and French, began to take a serious interest in the South Pacific region. By the end of the 18th century small British settlements existed in Australia and New Zealand. Thanks to fishing, farming (especially stock-raising) and gold mining, they grew into prosperous colonies.

*The Maoris tattooed their faces in elaborate patterns.*

## Aborigines

The first inhabitants of Australia, the ancestors of the Aborigines, arrived from south-east Asia about 20,000 years ago. The Aborigines varied in customs and appearance, so their ancestors may have been a mixture of peoples. In the 18th century the total Aboriginal population was probably about 300,000. Aboriginal culture was Stone Age, for they had no metals. They were hunters and gatherers of food, who lived in close sympathy with nature. In Western Australia, they lived in one of the harshest environments that human beings have ever inhabited. The way of life there was naturally different from that of people who lived in fertile regions, such as those of the south-east.

Most Europeans did not understand the Aborigines' way of life and treated them as less than human. More intelligent people, like Captain James Cook, admired their peacefulness but feared that their way of life was doomed. Cook was correct. European diseases, land-stealing and violence (in Tasmania the whole Aborigine race was destroyed) reduced the Aborigine population to less than 70,000 in under 100 years.

## Maoris

The Maoris of New Zealand were more recent arrivals. They were Polynesians, who came from other Pacific islands roughly 1,000 years ago, perhaps by following migrating birds. Maori culture was technologically more advanced than that of the Aborigines. They lived in well-built villages protected by strong forts, for they were a warlike people. They grew crops, made clothes, and had strong artistic traditions, especially wood carving. Although they had no writing, they had a spoken 'literature', a mixture of legends and history, which was passed down by teaching.

*To most Europeans, Aborigine society appeared simple. They saw naked people who ate insects. They failed to understand their close association with nature.*

## European settlement

The first British settlers in Australia were convicts, sent into exile instead of prison, who arrived in 1788. After early difficulties, the settlement prospered and attracted more colonists. British settlements grew, sheep farming proved profitable, and the land-hungry colonists steadily took over the country from the Aborigines, whose way of life was almost completely destroyed. The discovery of gold in 1851 resulted in a sharp increase in the European population, and by 1856 the larger Australian colonies had self-government under the British Crown. They eventually became states within a federation.

In New Zealand, unofficial European settlements arose on the coasts in the early 19th century. To enforce law and order, the British government appointed a governor (1840), who made an agreement with the Maoris that gave New Zealand to the British Crown in exchange for protection. The government, however, was too weak to prevent European settlers seizing Maori land. The result was war, and defeat for the Maoris. Relations later improved, but the Maoris are still trying to regain their land.

Below: *Convicts building the first settlement in Australia at Port Jackson, the site of one of today's great cities — Sydney.*

Right: *New Zealand was first surveyed thoroughly by Captain James Cook in 1769. At first the Maoris were hostile, but Cook later made friends with them. He greatly admired them for their sense of honour, and was impressed by their seamanship. Their biggest ocean-going canoes were longer than his own ship, which sailed around the world.*

# American Independence

Since the Renaissance of the 15th century, the rate of historical change in Europe had increased. Yet, after the disturbances of the 16th and 17th centuries, the pace of events seemed to slow down in the 18th century. At least, that is how it looks to us: people alive then probably did not think so. In the later part of the century, however, great upheavals did take place. The most obvious ones were political – changes in governments – although equally important developments were beginning in industry. These changes were both political and economic. They affected the future not only of Europe, but the whole world.

## United States

The people of Britain's 13 North American colonies resented the efforts of the British government to bring them under closer control after 1763. They objected especially to new taxes on trade, customs and excise duties. Like all taxation, these duties had been authorized by the British parliament. The American colonists complained that they had no representatives in that parliament. They demanded 'no taxation without representation'. The British government removed some of the objectionable taxes, but not all. Massachusetts colony was especially rebellious. After the Boston Tea Party (1773), the British government decided to get tough with Massachusetts. It passed laws to reduce the colony's independence (named by the colonists the 'Intolerable Acts'). The colonists began collecting guns. When a force of British soldiers tried to confiscate some guns being taken to Boston in 1775, shooting broke out. The Battle of Lexington, as the incident is called, marked the beginning of the colonists' war of independence.

Despite some differences, the 13 colonies managed to form a united opposition to Britain and in 1776 declared their independence. They set up a central government, the Continental Congress, and appointed George Washington commander-in-chief. The total population of the colonies was about 2 million, and their chances against mighty Britain looked poor. However, the Americans were skilful fighters and received help from France. Two British armies were forced to surrender, at Saratoga (1777) and Yorktown (1781), and in 1783 Britain recognized the independence of the United States of America.

*As a protest against a tax on tea, a party of rebels dressed as Amerindians went on board a British East India Company ship at Boston in 1773 and threw its cargo of tea into the harbour.*

The British used mercenaries in the forces sent to fight the rebels in America. Above left: A German trooper. Above: A colonial revolutionary.

Left: George Washington (1732–99) was a planter in Virginia who had some military service in colonial wars against the French and Amerindians. He led the American forces to victory in their war of independence and was elected first president of the United States (1789–97), afterwards retiring to his house, Mount Vernon, as a respected elder statesman.

## The US Constitution

A new kind of nation-state had come into the world. The Americans' Declaration of Independence stated that all men are created equal (slaves were not mentioned), that *the power of a government depends on the agreement of the people,* and that any government which denies its people the right to 'life, liberty and the pursuit of happiness' could be justly overthrown. A Bill of Rights was added to the constitution in 1791. It included the right to freedom of religion, freedom of speech, and freedom of the press.

The Americans distrusted powerful central governments, like the British one they had just broken free from, and they formed a federation of 13 states. Its constitution, drawn up in 1787, created a federal congress (parliament) of two houses, whose members were all elected. The federal government had the power to tax citizens and control trade, defence and foreign affairs, but each state also had its own government, its own elected assembly, and passed its own laws.

Below: The 'Founding Fathers' of the US Constitution produced a document to which all 13 states could agree. It is still the supreme law of the United States.

# French Revolution

The wars of the 17th and 18th centuries left France's royal government deeply in debt. The basic problem was that the wealthier classes, especially the very numerous nobility and clergy, paid practically no taxes, so the cost of government fell on poorer people. The small but growing middle class had no power. Attempts to reform the system, and end the privileges of the wealthy, stirred up so much opposition that the government feared to act. The eventual result was violent revolution (1789), which destroyed the French monarchy and undermined the idea that governments rule by right, not by consent of the people.

## The Enlightenment

The new way of looking at the world, now called the Enlightenment, grew out of the scientific advances of the 17th century. The philosophers of the Enlightenment believed that society could be improved by human reason and scientific knowledge. They criticized their own society, especially the influence of religion. Truth, they said, was not revealed by religious authority, but was reached by scientific reasoning. Doubt, said the great French philosopher Descartes, is the beginning of knowledge.

As knowledge advanced, ignorance would disappear and the world would become a better place. This was the belief of the thinkers of the Enlightenment, such as Denis Diderot and the authors of the French *Encyclopedia* (1751–72), the first attempt to summarize all human knowledge in one book.

Educated people recognized that they were living in an 'enlightened' age. Some European rulers, like Frederick the Great of Prussia, tried to put 'enlightened' policies into effect. Other people, especially those Frenchmen who had fought in the American Revolution, were influenced by the Americans' idea that governments ruled by consent, not by right.

Below: *During the Reign of Terror hundreds of people were executed by the guillotine, a beheading machine named after its inventor.*

The philosophes *were French intellectuals who spoke for the Enlightenment. They included: Voltaire (above), friend of Frederick the Great of Prussia; Rousseau, whose* Social Contract *placed the rights of citizens above the rights of government; and Diderot and the Encyclopedists.*

Above: *The Estates General consisted of nobility, clergy and 'Third Estate', representatives of the commoners. On 20 June 1789 the Third Estate, finding the doors of their assembly hall locked (by order of the King), assembled in the tennis court at Versailles, where they took an oath to stick together until France's new constitution was firmly established.*

## Liberty, equality, brotherhood

In 1789 the hard-pressed government of Louis XVI called an assembly of the Estates General, which included representatives of the commoners. It had not met since 1614. When the representatives met, they declared themselves a National Assembly, representing the sovereignty of the people. In two years it completely reformed the political and legal system, ending the privileges of the nobles and clergy and declaring all men equal in law. These reforms were very sensible, but they were carried out in an atmosphere of frantic excitement. The people of Paris, suffering from a famine, stormed the royal castle of the Bastille (14 July 1789), while in the countryside revolutionary groups took the lead in destroying many a noble's château. In 1793 a new and more extreme assembly created a republic and permitted a 'Reign of Terror' in which over 2,000 people were executed, including the King and Queen.

By 1799 France had made a complete break with her past. A complex society changed dramatically. Other European governments were frightened by the forces the Revolution had let loose. War had broken out with Austria and Prussia, who were believed to be on the point of interfering in French affairs, in 1792. The Revolution had become a European event, for the ideals of 'liberty, equality and brotherhood' could be exported. The division of modern European politics into liberal and conservative can be said to date from this time.

*The French Revolution began when the people of Paris stormed the Bastille in 1789.*

# Napoleon

Between 1789 and 1799 a series of different political groups dominated government in France. The last revolutionary government, the Directory (1795–99), was overthrown in a plot which brought a popular young general, Napoleon Bonaparte (1769–1821), to power. For 15 years this remarkable man dominated Europe.

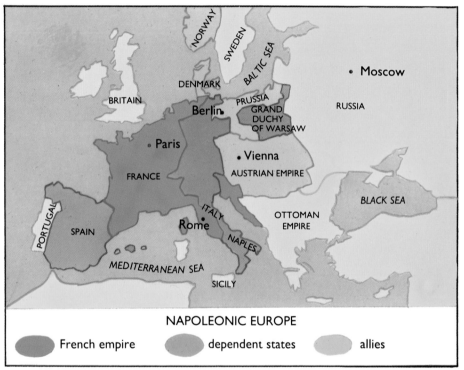

NAPOLEONIC EUROPE

French empire          dependent states          allies

## Napoleon Bonaparte

Napoleon became the conqueror of Europe. He was in effect a dictator, being crowned emperor of France in 1804. He sometimes imprisoned people without trial (like the old royal government) and he reimposed censorship, which had ended in the Revolution. However, Napoleon himself was a son of the Revolution, and a believer in most of its ideas. His conquests spread those ideas across Europe and encouraged the two new forces which were to dominate politics in the 19th century – nationalism and liberalism. In some ways Napoleon carried the Revolution further. The Napoleonic Code, a new and very thorough system of law, was introduced not only in France but in much of mainland Europe. Other reforms were no less important. Education, economic affairs (including the introduction of the metric system) and political administration were all shaken up, reformed, and brought under more efficient, central control.

## Napoleonic Europe

In the long run, such reforms proved more important than Napoleon's sensational military victories. The reason for his wars was largely the hostility of other nations towards France and her revolutionary influence, but partly also the result of Napoleon's ambition. Thanks to his own ability and the fighting power of France's revolutionary armies, which were made up of citizens, not mercenaries, Napoleon conquered most of Europe with great ease, setting up his brothers as kings. Although his empire did not last long, it caused some permanent changes in Europe. For

## TIMETABLE

1789  Outbreak of French Revolution
1792  France declared a republic; war with Austria and Prussia
1793  King and Queen executed; Reign of Terror; war with Britain
1799  Napoleon seizes power; renewed war against European powers
1800  French victories against Austria (Marengo, Hohenlinden)
1804  Napoleon crowned emperor
1805  Battle of Trafalgar; French victory at Austerlitz
1806  Prussia defeated; French in Berlin and Warsaw
1807  Russians defeated; Rome occupied
1808  French invade Spain and Portugal; Peninsular War begins
1812  Russia invaded
1813  Napoleon defeated in 'Battle of the Nations' (Leipzig)
1814  Allies invade France; Napoleon exiled to island of Elba; Congress of Vienna meets
1815  Napoleon escapes; defeated at Waterloo; sent to St Helena

*Napoleon Bonaparte was crowned the first emperor of France in 1804.*

## NAPOLEON'S EMPIRE

Napoleon was a man of extraordinary abilities. He had a huge capacity for work and a vast supply of emotional energy. Above all, he was a born leader. Though a small man, he seemed to radiate power like an electric charge.

In 1812 Napoleon invaded Russia. He reached Moscow, but lost 500,000 men during the retreat.

example, it brought the Holy Roman Empire to an end in 1806, and swept away most of the little German states that had been able to cling to their independence since the Middle Ages.

Napoleonic France had some weaknesses. On land, the French armies were almost unbeatable, but the British ruled the seas, and Napoleon had to give up plans to invade England even before the combined French and Spanish fleets were defeated at Trafalgar in 1805. More important, Napoleon had too many enemies. His decision to invade Russia in 1812 proved a fatal mistake. His army was destroyed in the cruel winter weather, and in 1814 the combined powers of Europe forced him to abdicate. He made a startling comeback a few months later, but suffered his greatest, final defeat at Waterloo (1815).

*After his defeat at Waterloo on 18 June 1815, Napoleon Bonaparte was held captive on the tiny island of St Helena, in the Atlantic Ocean, 2,000km (1,200 miles) off the west coast of southern Africa. He died there in 1821.*

After Napoleon's defeat the statesmen of Europe met at the Congress of Vienna to settle Europe's affairs. They restored the monarchy in France, and would have liked to restore everything else to its position of 1789. In the long run, this was impossible. The forces of change let loose between 1789 and 1815 could not be crushed. The 'old regime' in Europe had been destroyed and, in spite of the apparent victory of conservatism at Vienna, it could never be restored.

# References

**Almohads** Muslim dynasty based in Morocco, controlling much of north-west Africa and Spain in the 12th and 13th centuries, which spread Islam in West Africa.

**Bantu** A term for most peoples in Africa south of the Sahara, speaking similar languages and with similar customs.

**Boers** A name meaning 'farmers' given to the mainly Dutch colonists in South Africa and their Afrikaner descendants.

**Boer War** (or South African War, 1899–1902) A war between British and Boers caused by competition for gold and diamonds in Transvaal and the Boers' desire for independence.

**Cook, James** (1728–79) English navigator who explored New Zealand and eastern Australia (1768–71), circled Antarctica (1772–75), and rediscovered Hawaii (1778).

**Descartes, René** (1596–1650) French philosopher and mathematician, one of the greatest figures in establishing modern philosophy and scientific thought.

**Directory** The government of France, 1795–99, which formed an interval between revolutionary extremism and Napoleon's takeover.

**Dissenters** The name given to those who 'dissented' from (disagreed with) the practice and organization of the Church of England.

**'Enlightened despots'** A name given to certain 18th century rulers, including Frederick the Great and Joseph II of Austria, who held absolute power but governed according to the ideas of the Enlightenment philosophers.

**Frederick II, the Great** (1712–86) King of Prussia (from 1740) who made Prussia a great power in Europe through war abroad and good government at home.

**French and Indian War** The name by which the Seven Years' War is known in North America.

**Girondins** A French revolutionary party in 1791–93, less radical than the Jacobins; they planned to arrest Jacobin leaders in 1793, but were themselves arrested.

**Great Trek** The movement of a large number of Boers beginning in 1835, from Cape Colony across the Orange and Vaal rivers, to establish free republics.

**Huron** A federation of Amerindian nations, based mainly in Ontario, who were generally hostile to the Iroquois and friendly towards the French.

**Indians** (or 'Red Indians') A popular name for the first inhabitants of North America, now called Amerindians or native Americans.

**Iroquois** (or the Five Nations) A federation of Amerindians dominant in what is now the north-east United States and south-east Canada, generally friendly to the British and hostile to the French in the 18th century.

**Jacobins** Extremist French revolutionary party, led by Maximilien de Robespierre (1758–94), dominant 1793–94 and responsible for the Reign of Terror.

**Jefferson, Thomas** (1743–1826) US president (1801–09) who drafted the Declaration of Independence (1776) and was an important influence on the US Constitution.

**Louisiana** A vast territory of North America, stretching from Oregon and Minnesota to the Gulf of Mexico, claimed by France from 1682, and sold to the United States in 1803; its purchase greatly encouraged westward expansion.

**New England** The north-east United States, today containing the states of Maine, Vermont, New Hampshire, Massachusetts, Connecticut and Rhode Island.

**Peninsular War** A series of campaigns, 1808–14, in which British forces led by the Duke of Wellington, with Portuguese and Spanish help, drove French troops out of most of the Iberian peninsula.

**Pilgrim Fathers** The name given to the first English settlers in New England, a group of Dissenters who sailed in the *Mayflower* to found the colony of Plymouth, Massachusetts, in 1620.

**Polynesians** The inhabitants of a large group of Pacific islands, including New Zealand, Hawaii and Tahiti.

**Pombal, Marquis de** (1699–1782) Portuguese statesman and near-dictator from the 1750s to 1777, who developed the colony of Brazil but, by expelling the Jesuits, encouraged further exploitation of the Amerindians by white settlers.

**Seven Years' War** A European conflict, 1756–63, in which Britain and Prussia were allied against France, Austria, Spain and Russia, resulting in gains for Britain in trade and colonies, and the recognition of Prussia as a great European power.

**Virginia** The name of the territory in North America first colonized by the English (1607); in the 17th century the name was given to the whole area of English interest in North America, not just the present state.

**Waitangi, Treaty of** An agreement of 1840 between the Maoris and the newly appointed British governor of New Zealand, granting sovereignty to Britain in exchange for protection of Maori lands and fisheries.

**Washington, George** (1732–99) US president (1789–97), elected commander-in-chief of forces against the British (1775); retired to his plantation at Mount Vernon after British defeat until called to office (1787).

**Wellington, Duke of** (1769–1852) British general and prime minister (1828–30) who conducted the Peninsular War against French forces and commanded the main allied army which, with Marshal Blücher's Prussians, defeated Napoleon at Waterloo (1815).

# *The Industrial Revolution*

# Machines and Factories

Since the Middle Ages, Europe had been growing richer as trade, industry and population all expanded. In the late 18th century economic progress suddenly began to speed up dramatically. In the next 100 years, Western society was completely changed. These startling economic changes are together known as the Industrial Revolution – a revolution that affected people's lives no less than political revolution. The Industrial Revolution marks the last great spurt in the rate of change in human society. Since 1800 life in Western countries has changed faster than at any other time, and that speed of change so far shows no sign of slowing down.

## Capital and the market

The Industrial Revolution introduced a new type of economy, which was dominated by market forces – buying and selling.

Trade grew rapidly in the 18th century: the volume of trade in France in 1789 was five times greater than it was in 1715. The profits of trade helped to create capital – money for investment. Much of this capital was invested in land, but industry and banking benefited too. In most countries, one bank, like the Bank of England, not only financed the government but also controlled national financial affairs and issued banknotes. The activities of bankers helped to create a more international economy. A worker in England, for example, might find himself out of work as a result of a bank failure in America.

*The 'scientific revolution' of the 17th century resulted in technological advances, such as accurate clocks controlled by a pendulum. But precision-engineering technology lagged behind science until the 19th century.*

## Mass production

The most obvious feature of the Industrial Revolution was the production of goods by machines in factories. Machines need power, and that was provided by burning coal to make steam. The main industrial regions were usually near coalfields, such as South Wales, the Ruhr valley and Silesia.

Machines took over jobs traditionally done by people at home. Inventions came thick and fast. For example, in the British cotton industry, the

*Left: Large new textile mills revolutionized the British cotton industry.*

flying shuttle (1733) made weaving much faster. Spinning lagged behind until the spinning jenny appeared. One step led to another: the water frame and the spinning mule left weaving once more lagging, until the invention of the power loom (1785). Mechanization was applied in the fields too: the cotton gin (1793) made cotton-picking much faster.

Under the old production system, spinners and weavers had worked mainly in their own cottages. The new power-driven machines made it necessary to gather all workers in one place. Work was more disciplined. Workers had to keep regular hours, and the machines dictated the rate of work. Foremen and managers supervized the workers. Production increased enormously. A steam-driven spinning mule, tended by two or three people, could do the work of 100 hand spinners.

Some industries grew equally fast without mechanization. Mining needed pumps (powered by the steam engine) and good transport, provided from the 1840s by railways. But the method of producing coal did not change much. The difference was that far more miners were employed. A few thousands in 1800 had grown to many millions by 1900.

*Right: A steel furnace. In the early 18th century it became possible to make iron cheaply by using coal, not charcoal, in blast furnaces. Cheap steel had to wait for the invention of the Bessemer process in 1856.*

| SCIENTIFIC DISCOVERIES AND INVENTIONS 1750–1900 | |
| --- | --- |
| 1752 Lightning conductor | Franklin (Pennsylvania) |
| 1769 Efficient steam engine | Watt (Britain) |
| 1772 Nature of combustion (burning) | Lavoisier (France) |
| 1783 Hot-air balloon | Montgolfiers (France) |
| 1786 Steamboat | Fitch (USA) |
| 1800 Electric battery | Volta (Italy) |
| 1808 Combining of gases | Gay-Lussac (France) |
| 1820 Electromagnetism | Oersted (Denmark) |
| 1820 Force between electric currents | Ampère (France) |
| 1822 Photograph | Niepce (France) |
| 1827 Law of electric current | Ohm (Germany) |
| 1831 Electric transformer and dynamo | Faraday (Britain) |
| 1837 Electric telegraph | Cooke, Wheatstone (Britain) |
| 1856 Steel furnace | Bessemer (Britain) |
| 1862 Plastics | Parkes (Britain) |
| 1867 Dynamite | Nobel (Sweden) |
| 1876 Telephone | Bell (USA) |
| 1879 Electric light | Edison (USA) |
| 1885 Motor car | Benz (Germany) |
| 1887 Radio waves | Hertz (Germany) |
| 1894 Radio transmitter/receiver | Marconi (Italy) |
| 1895 X-rays | Röntgen (Germany) |
| 1896 Radioactivity | Becquerel (France) |
| 1897 Electron | Thomson (Britain) |
| 1900 Quantum theory | Planck (Germany) |

# Industrial Cities

The Industrial Revolution changed the European landscape. The most obvious change was the growth of cities. Between 1800 and 1900 many a sleepy market town turned into a sprawling metropolis. This produced many severe social problems. A French visitor to Manchester, one of the earliest industrial cities, exclaimed with horror, "Civilized man is turned back almost into a savage." Riots and even rebellions were common signs of people's distress. After about 1850, however, living standards improved and outbreaks of violence declined.

## Workers and bosses

The aim of industrial society was profit. Nothing was allowed to interfere with that, and factory owners believed that profits would be greater if wages were kept low.

The living conditions of the new, industrial working class were grim. People were crowded into slums, with no lighting except candles and no running water. Working hours were long; twelve hours a day, six days a week. Factories were dangerous, noisy and badly ventilated. There were no paid holidays, no insurance against illness or unemployment, and trade unions were illegal. The work was often dangerous and nearly always dull. Each person did the same small job in the manufacturing process, hour after hour, day after day. Very young children, who never went to school, worked at the simpler jobs in factories and mines.

Despite these hardships, living conditions for many people in the new industrial cities were perhaps no worse than living conditions in the country, and conditions did slowly improve. What was new was the size of the problem. The industrial cities grew without plan. Outsiders looked at the teeming millions of poor workers with astonishment, horror and fear. The poor, dirty, uneducated city masses were a strange new feature of society, perhaps a source of revolution. People's resentment sometimes boiled over into violence, yet until 1829 no European country had a regular police force. Soldiers controlled riots.

## POPULATION GROWTH

Even before 1800 some people were worried by Europe's fast-growing population, but in the 19th century it grew even faster. Although millions of Europeans emigrated to North America, Australia and other places, the European population rose from about 180 million in 1800 to about 400 million in 1900. One reason for this growth was improvements in farming, which increased food production. Another was the decline in the death rate as a result of better hygiene (cleaner water, proper sewers) and medicine.

*An industrial city in Britain, 'the workshop of the world' and leading country in the Industrial Revolution.*

*On farms, children had always worked as soon as they were old enough, but the idea of children under ten working in mines and factories was more shocking.*

## Reform

The problems were so huge that the only authority powerful enough to solve them was the government. However, it had never been the job of government to make laws for social welfare. The then current belief in the principle of *laissez-faire*, which means letting things alone, made governments very reluctant to interfere.

However, under pressure from social reformers, they were forced to act. Laws were passed limiting hours of work, laying down minimum standards for housing and places of work, and banning child labour. Trade unions became legal.

By the end of the 19th century some governments had introduced social welfare programmes such as sickness benefit. Great advances were starting to be made in public health. Organized rubbish collection and the construction of proper sewers and drains brought to an end epidemics of diseases like cholera, which had swept through cities killing tens of thousands of people.

During the last half of the century, riots were fewer and anti-government rebellions less successful. Higher wages and living standards explain this improvement. The Industrial Revolution began by making a few people rich while keeping millions poor. In time, though it did not reduce the gap between rich and poor, it did make even the poor comparatively richer.

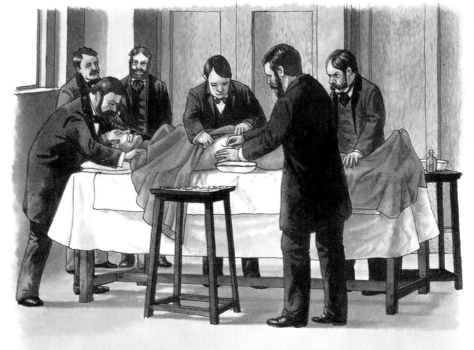

*Medicine was still crude in the early 19th century. Operations still often had to be done without anaesthetics.*

# Railway Age

In 1800 transport was slow and expensive. It took two weeks for news from Italy to reach England, two months for it to reach North America. Goods took even longer to move. The Industrial Revolution would have soon faltered without faster and cheaper transport, especially overland. As in other industries, the first step was to improve the current system. Canals were built to link cities and coal mines with rivers and the sea (50,000km of canals were dug in Britain alone between 1760 and 1830). Roads were improved, and so were horse-drawn coaches. This was not enough. The answer to the transport problem proved to be the steam-driven locomotive running on iron rails.

*George Stephenson's Rocket, built in 1829, heralded the age of the steam train.*

### Early railways
Wooden rails, carrying waggons drawn by horses, had long been used in mines. Public railways became possible with the development of reliable iron rails and steam locomotives. The first, the Stockton–Darlington Railway in the industrial north of England, opened in 1825. It used horses and stationary steam engines (which drew the train uphill by a chain), as well as locomotives. The success of George Stephenson's locomotives, which ran on the Liverpool–Manchester Railway (1830) was decisive in the future of railways.

### The world on rails
Though the noisy monsters were unpopular with landowners, farmers and coach travellers (because steam locomotives frightened the horses), businessmen and governments quickly recognized the importance of railways.

Belgium kept its historic position as a crossroads of European trade by building a state railway system which linked Brussels with the ports and connected with French and Prussian railways. British engineers, the pioneers of railway construction, were soon hard at work all over the world.

Railways enabled industry to develop at a great rate. They made possible vast engineering businesses, like the Krupp works in Essen, Germany. In France, railways carried food cheaply from farming to industrial regions.

In the United States, a land of huge distances, railways brought immigrants to settle in new regions. Railways were also used to transport minerals from places that had previously been too far away to exploit. The booming oil industry was a direct offspring of the arrival of the railways.

After 1850 the railways, along with coal, iron and steel, which kept them (and the new steamships) going, were the leading industry. Many thousands of people grew rich (and some lost everything they had) through frantic buying and selling of shares in railway companies.

**Communications**
A new industrial society, with big businesses and international banking, needed faster communications as well as transport. The railways carried mail for the post office, and an international postal service was created in 1875. Advances in the study of electromagnetism led to the first form of 'instant' communication, the telegraph, which transmitted messages by cable in Morse code. Better still were the telephone, which allowed two-way communication, and radio, which did not depend on cables. Rapid communications encouraged a huge growth in newspapers and the ability to pass messages instantly changed the way wars were fought. Warfare was also changed enormously by the introduction of conscripted 'citizen-armies' and by new weapons such as the machine gun and the explosive shell.

*Railways, built with great speed, linked the east and west coasts of the United States from 1869. To secure grants of land from the federal government, companies built railways in areas not yet settled by whites.*

SHIPPING

Though steam engines were first used in ships before 1800, iron-hulled steamers did not begin to take over from wooden sailing ships until the development of the screw propeller, in about 1840. The growth of trade, the building of canals, especially the Suez Canal (opened 1869), and the creation of coaling stations in distant places were all part of the rapid growth of shipping and shipbuilding.

Canals carried barges across valleys, on aqueducts, and through mountains, in tunnels. But the canal age was short: railways soon took over the transportation of bulky goods.

# American Civil War

One of the most important 19th century developments for the future of the world was the rise of the United States. In 1800 it was still a small country of about 5 million people, most of whom lived along the Atlantic coast. By 1900 it was the richest nation in the world, ahead of Britain in trade and industry, and with a fast-growing population of 76 million. It had many advantages; the most important the wealth of the land itself. Most countries were mainly manufacturers, like Britain, or producers, like Australia. The United States, with its rich natural resources, was both.

*Abraham Lincoln (born 1809) led the North to victory in the Civil War. He was assassinated in 1865.*

## North and South

The greatest threat to the United States came from within. The country was not firmly united. The sharpest division lay between the agricultural South and industrial North. The South depended on slavery for its wealth – by this time chiefly cotton – while most Northerners, who had no slaves, believed slavery should be abolished or at least not allowed to spread. The Republican Party, founded in 1855, stood firm against allowing slavery in the new states and territories of the West. When a Republican, Abraham Lincoln, was elected president in 1860, the Southern states announced that they were withdrawing from the union to form an independent nation.

## War for the Union

Lincoln's government refused to accept this decision to split the country in two, and the result was civil war. The North had many advantages: it had twice as many people, more money, most of the factories, and the navy, which prevented the South receiving help from abroad. But the people of the South had great fighting spirit and excellent generals, and the war lasted four years (1861–65) before the South was forced to surrender. The war brought slavery to an end. In 1863 Abraham Lincoln proclaimed emancipation (freedom) for all slaves. Blacks were still treated as 'second-class citizens' for 100 years after the war, but they were 'free', if not 'equal'.

*Left: Nearly 1 million men were killed in the American Civil War.*

## Wealth and poverty

The prosperity of the United States boomed after the Civil War. Immigrants flocked in from Europe. The western lands filled up with settlers, and the farmland of the Middle West became Europe's 'bread basket'. Small forts and trading posts grew into cities. Railways snaked across the country. Oil wells, steel plants and mining towns sprang up, followed by new industries based on oil, electricity and plastics. Americans took the lead in technology and in new, aggressive business methods.

Not everyone did well, not the blacks, nor many of the poor in the cities, nor the peasant farmers of the South, and certainly not the original inhabitants. The Amerindians were simply pushed aside by the tide of settlers. Bitter frontier wars were fought against Cheyenne, Sioux and other nations, which ended with the defeated Amerindians being crowded into reservations. Cattle and corn fields filled up the plains where once wild bison herds had roamed.

Above: *Blacks in the South celebrate the Emancipation Proclamation, ending slavery.*

Below: *Waggon trains carried thousands of poor people (many of them recent arrivals from Europe) to a new life in towns and settlements of the American West.*

# Nationalism

The two great driving forces of political change in the 19th century were liberalism and nationalism. A 'state' was a man-made thing. A 'nation' seemed more natural. The idea of a 'nation' was based on language. 'Whenever a separate language is found,' wrote the German philosopher Johann Fichte, 'there is also a separate nation which has the right...to rule itself.' Nationalism – the desire to get rid of alien rulers and set up an independent state – was one of the reasons for the many riots and rebellions of 1820–48 in Europe.

## War and revolt

The Congress of Vienna had tried to restore the map of Europe to the situation of 1789. This settlement could not last. Civil war in the Netherlands resulted in the creation of a separate kingdom of Belgium (1839). The revolt of the Greeks (Orthodox Christians) against Turkish (Muslim) rule, which began in 1821, ended in an independent Greece in 1830. In the same year, a revolt led by army officers began in Poland against Russian rule. But this was a nationalist revolt that failed. Unlike most countries of Western Europe, Poland had no large, liberal, middle class; the peasants were unwilling to cooperate with the landowners, and the Poles received no help from Britain or France, the two liberal powers of Europe, which were sympathetic to nationalism. The Polish rebellion was crushed.

## Italy

In 1820 Italy was divided into four. The north was ruled by Austria; the south (the Kingdom of the Two Sicilies) was ruled by a Bourbon dynasty. The small kingdom of Sardinia and the Papal States were independent. After earlier disturbances, Italy's revolution began in 1848. This was the 'Year of Revolution', when most European countries had some kind of uprising. Rebellion in Italy was quickly followed by revolts of other subjects of the Austrian empire, such as the Czechs and Hungarians. The revolt in Italy was suppressed, but only temporarily. Revolutionaries turned to politics and diplomacy, and the lead was taken by Count Cavour (1810–61), who gained the support of France. In 1860 another Italian nationalist hero, Garibaldi, led a revolt in the south. The French defeated the Austrians, Garibaldi overthrew the Bourbon monarchy, and the Sardinian army marched into the Papal States to meet him. Italy was united as one kingdom.

Right: *Garibaldi leads his 'Red Shirt' followers in southern Italy.*

## Germany

The old Habsburg empire of Austria was in a weak position in an age of nationalism because it contained so many people eager to be free. Austria kept Hungary only by creating a dual monarchy; in Germany it lost its dominance to Prussia.

Germany was still divided into many small states. Although nationalist ambition for unity was strong, the numerous customs barriers hindered trade and development. Prussia took the lead in forming a customs union, or 'common market'. Led by Bismarck, Prussia gained Schleswig-Holstein from Denmark. Bismarck then fashioned a convenient quarrel with Austria, which was defeated (1866) in just four weeks. The French, frightened by looming Prussian power, unwisely declared war in 1870. They were heavily defeated, and Prussia gained Alsace-Lorraine. The new provinces were handed over, not to Prussia, but to a new German Empire, which came into official existence in 1871.

### IRELAND

Ireland had come under English rule since the Middle Ages. It was a poor country, and its people were Roman Catholics, unlike the Protestant British, who owned most of the land. In 1845–49 a terrible famine, resulting from the failure of the potato crop, reduced the population by a quarter. Some people died, while many emigrated. After about 1870, the British made some long-needed reforms, but the Irish wanted independence. They won it finally, after guerilla war, in 1921, though Protestant Northern Ireland remained British.

A vast new power had been created. Bismarck resigned in 1890, but the empire he had created proved to have still greater ambitions for expansion.

Right: *Bismarck (1815–1898), the 'Iron Chancellor'.*
Below: *William I of Prussia was crowned Emperor of Germany at Versailles in 1871.*

### THE RISE OF JAPAN

| | |
|---|---|
| 1867 | Meiji emperor restored; rapid industrial advance; modern navy and army created |
| 1894–95 | War with China; gains include Taiwan |
| 1902 | Alliance with Britain; Japan's navy third largest |
| 1904–05 | War with Russia; gains include southern Manchuria |
| 1910 | Korea annexed |

# Western Powers

In the 19th century the West – Europe and North America – became richer and therefore more powerful. By the end of the century, much of the world, including all of Africa and India, was ruled directly by European powers. Even those countries not under European rule were dominated by European ideas and by European interests. Most are to this day, for although the West no longer rules half the world, Western ideas of economic progress and democratic government have become the universal aim of world society. Even the most dictatorial governments usually pretend to be 'democratic'.

## Great power rivalry

World history in the 19th century was dominated by events in Europe. Europe consisted of several powerful, jealous, or nervous rivals. Politicians worried about keeping the 'balance of power': no single country should be allowed to grow too great. If it threatened to do so, others hastened to form an alliance to stop it. The British were especially keen on maintaining the balance of power, but did not apply the rule to sea power (the British navy was unchallenged).

One of the chief threats to the balance of power arose from the weakness of the Turkish empire. This gave subject peoples like the Greeks, Serbs and Bulgarians a chance to assert their nationalism. More dangerously, it invited interference from the great powers, especially Russia. Russian ambitions in the region led to the Crimean War (1854–56), the first European war since the defeat of Napoleon. Russia was checked, but the problem remained. The international Congress of Berlin (1878) settled European affairs for a time, but the next major crisis in the region was to end in world war.

Below: *One effect of the Industrial Revolution in Europe was to create a large, prosperous, politically powerful middle class.*

Right: *By the end of the 19th century, most Western countries had introduced compulsory primary education for all children. This was one of the most important results of the growing concern of governments with social reform.*

## Russia

Though still a comparatively backward country, liberalism and nationalism influenced Russia also. The government of the tsar tried to make use of nationalist feelings by emphasizing the brotherhood of the Slav peoples; this helped extend its influence to south-east Europe. Russia was unstable. There was much violence in the countryside and political plotting in the towns, and the need for reform was widely recognized. In 1861 serfdom, which lay at the root of Russia's problems, was at last abolished. This was a costly step, and the ex-serfs were little better off, owing to high rents and small plots. Other reforms followed, including more democratic government and equality of all subjects in law. But they came too late. The threat of violent revolution still lay over Russia.

Above: *The bicycle became popular in the 1870s. Early tyres were solid, giving a bumpy ride.*

## France

Monarchy in France was overthrown again in 1848. Napoleon's nephew was elected president, but in 1851 he abolished the national assembly and declared himself emperor, as Napoleon III ('Napoleon II' had never reigned). For several years he was a great figure in Europe, the champion of liberalism who made the uniting of Italy easier by defeating the Austrians. But times had changed. Industrialization had increased demands for social reform, or even socialist government, and Napoleon III never recovered from France's defeat by Prussia in 1870. He went into exile in England.

In Paris, the bitterness of the people led to the creation of a revolutionary movement known as the Commune, which controlled the city for two months in 1871 before it was crushed with savage violence. A republican government was restored which, in spite of the fierce political divisions in France, managed to survive until the First World War.

### MARX AND DARWIN

The two most influential thinkers of the 19th century were Karl Marx (1818–83) and Charles Darwin (1809–82). Marx was the founder of Communism. He believed that capitalist society would be destroyed by a revolution of the working class. Darwin was a biologist who explained (in *On the Origin of Species*, 1859) how evolution works. This scientific explanation of life seemed to deny the existence of God the creator.

*Karl Marx*

*Charles Darwin*

# European Empires

During the 19th century, when the wealth and power of Europe dominated the world, large parts of Asia and Africa came under direct European rule for the first time. This was an unexpected and even an unwanted development. In South America, by contrast, European rule was ending, not beginning. Britain gained the largest world empire, yet it had lost its enthusiasm for colonies since the United States became independent. Many colonies were seized simply to prevent a European rival getting them, and thus upsetting the balance of power or threatening Britain's rule of the seas. But colonies once gained were not easily given up.

## India

The British were not enthusiastic about most of their colonies, but India was an exception. By 1850, the East India Company had become, in effect, the government of India. It introduced laws and education based on the British pattern. English became the official language, and missionaries preached the Christian religion. The ruling class was entirely British.

In 1857 a widespread revolt broke out against the British among people angered by the damage done to traditional Indian culture. The revolt was suppressed, and the immediate result was the ending of the company's authority (and of the Mughal dynasty) in favour of direct rule by Britain. A more important result was growing hostility between British and Indians, made worse by imports of cheap British manufactures that hampered the development of Indian industry.

THE DELHI DURBAR

The Delhi Durbar was a public audience presided over by the British Viceroy. It symbolized the curious relationship between Britain and India. Many British people in India became more Indian than British, while those who understood nothing of Indian culture enjoyed the luxuries of Indian princely society. Feelings of racial superiority were rare among the British until the 19th century, when they came to believe the myths about their own power and achievements.

## The Dominions

In British-ruled countries like Australia, Canada and New Zealand, the native people were fewer in number and had little power or influence. They had no choice but to accept British culture. In those countries and in South Africa, the immigrants and their descendants took over. They became self-governing dominions, independent but still within the British empire.

## The imperial powers

France also increased her empire enormously, especially in North and West Africa, the Middle East and south-east Asia. Other European nations followed the British and French example. The most remarkable feature of this empire-building was the 'scramble' for Africa. Almost the whole continent came under European rule at the end of the 19th century.

The people of the United States, although ex-colonists who disliked imperial power, also extended their territories. They took over Hawaii; made Cuba a US dependency; imposed direct rule on Puerto Rico and the Philippines; and created a puppet republic in Panama, so that they could build and operate the Panama Canal themselves.

This carve-up of the world took place with relatively little violence and for a strange mixture of reasons. The greed of businessmen, the hopes of emigrants, the ambitions of

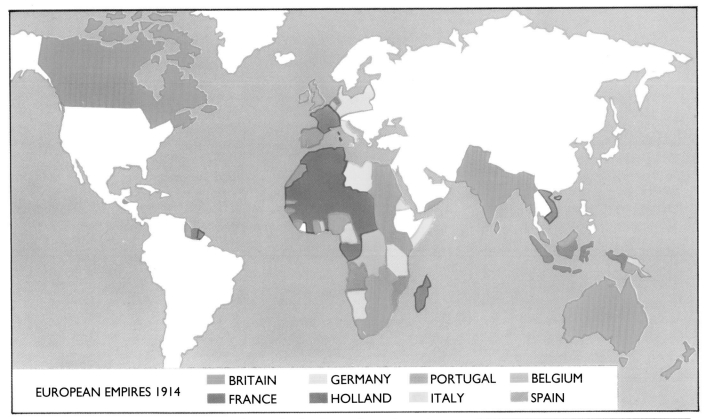

**EUROPEAN EMPIRES 1914**

- BRITAIN
- FRANCE
- GERMANY
- HOLLAND
- PORTUGAL
- ITALY
- BELGIUM
- SPAIN

missionaries and explorers, the desire to guard against supposed threats from rivals – and the simple feeling that if other countries had colonies *we* should have them too – all played their part. Many Europeans felt they were carrying out an important duty by bringing 'the blessings of civilization' to less fortunate people. Those people may have had other ideas, but they were seldom asked. Europeans felt they knew best.

There was a logical outcome. When, for example, an African child learned about 'freedom, equality and brotherhood' from French teachers, he soon began to reason that, if such ideas were right for Frenchmen, they should be right for Africans, too!

### CRISIS AT FASHODA

The European powers acquired their overseas empires without war between themselves, although there were occasional crises when their ambitions clashed. At Fashoda (Kodok) on the upper Nile, a French force from the west confronted a rival British force from the north in 1898. War was avoided when the French agreed to leave the Nile valley to Britain.

Below: *Great ocean steamers made transatlantic travel much faster.*

# References

**Alsace-Lorraine**  Northern provinces of France, disputed between France and Germany, held by Germany 1871–1918 and 1940–44.

**Bismarck, Prince Otto von** (1815–98) Prussian statesman and first chancellor of Germany (1871–90) who brought about the unification of Germany and was the dominant European statesman in the last quarter of the 19th century.

**Capitalism**  The economic system in which the production and marketing of goods, together with financing and investment, are owned by private persons or companies whose motive is profit.

**Carpetbaggers**  A name given to US Northerners, who went south after the Civil War and, as the old Southern ruling class was not allowed to hold office, dominated Southern politics until about 1872.

**Confederates**  Southerners in the American Civil War.

**Crimean War**  A war (1854–56) in which Russia was opposed by France, Britain and Turkey, begun mainly as a result of fears of Russian expansion in south-east Europe and fought in the Crimean Peninsula on the Black Sea.

**Death rate**  The number of deaths in a fixed time as a proportion of the whole population; in 1800 the death rate in Europe was about 35 per thousand per year, but by 1900 only about 28 per thousand.

**Dominion**  The name, meaning the power of governing, given to those countries of the British Empire, or Commonwealth, which had self-government but remained under the British Crown.

**Dual Monarchy**  Austria and Hungary, which had separate governments under the Habsburg emperor, 1867–1918.

**Free trade**  The idea that goods traded between different countries should not have to pay customs duties or similar taxes; free trade was especially popular in 19th century Britain.

**Garibaldi, Giuseppe** (1807–82) Italian nationalist, who organized the expedition of 1,000 men (known as 'Red Shirts') that overthrew the King of the Two Sicilies in 1860, a victory leading to the unification of Italy.

**Gettysburg, Battle of**  The greatest battle of the American Civil War (1863), won by the North but at heavy cost in lives; famous also as the site of President Lincoln's 'Gettysburg Address' four months later, in which he defended the principles of the US Constitution.

**Liberalism**  The belief in a set of connected ideas such as more democratic government, freedom of speech and religion, *laissez-faire* government, and free trade; it owed something to the Enlightenment and something to the tradition of civil liberties in Britain.

**Lincoln, Abraham** (1809–65) US president (1861–65), whose election caused Southern states to leave the Union, resulting in the Civil War; he was assassinated five days after the war ended.

**Luddites**  A name given to English workers in the Industrial Revolution who broke up machines as a protest against losing their jobs; the name came from a legendary leader, Ned Ludd.

**Mexican War**  US name for the war (1846–48) between the United States and Mexico by which the United States gained Texas, New Mexico and part of California.

**Monroe Doctrine**  A principle of US foreign policy declared by President Monroe in 1823, that no interference in North or South America by European powers should be allowed.

**Morse, Samuel** (1791–1872) US inventor of the Morse Code for sending messages by telegraph, who sent the first telegram, from Washington to Baltimore: 'What hath God wrought!'

**Nightingale, Florence** (1820–1910) English hospital reformer, who nursed the wounded in the Crimean War, gaining the nickname 'The Lady with the Lamp', and later established the modern nursing profession in Britain.

**Railway mania**  The craze for railway schemes and companies, many of them quite impracticable, and for buying shares in such companies, first experienced in England in the 1830s.

**Raj**  A name, meaning 'kingdom' in Hindi, given to the British Indian empire (not to the whole British empire).

**Risorgimento**  The movement for Italian unification in the 19th century, which ended successfully in 1861 (except for Venice and Rome, added later).

**Romantic movement**  A trend in European culture in the 19th century, giving greater importance to imagination and feelings; it was sympathetic to nationalism.

**Smith, Adam** (1723–90)  Scottish economist, author of *The Wealth of Nations* (1776), which first defined the modern capitalist system, defining wealth as the product of labour, and upholding free trade and individual enterprise.

**Socialism**  The system, opposed to capitalism, in which the means of production and distribution (farms, factories, shops) belong to the whole society, not to private people or companies.

**Stephenson, George** (1781–1848) British engineer, builder of the first successful steam locomotives and railways; with his son Robert (1803–59) he later built railways and engines for other countries.

**Unionists**  Northerners, or supporters of the Union, in the American Civil War.

**Watt, James** (1736–1819) Scottish engineer who invented a much improved steam engine, suitable for driving machines, in the 1760s.

# The Age of Destruction

# The First World War

At the end of the 19th century, the world was as peaceful as it ever had been. World order, controlled by the Western powers, depended on stability in Europe. In 1914 that order and stability broke down and the world was plunged into war, the first major war in Europe for 100 years. Fought by large armies of conscripted men, with the deadly weapons of industrialized society, the war proved more destructive than anyone had imagined.

*The horror of trench warfare.*

## Causes

The European policy of keeping a 'balance of power' had disastrous results. Nervous of each other, nations hurried to form defensive alliances for their own security. Between 1879 and 1907, this system of alliances turned Europe into two armed camps – Germany and Austria-Hungary on one side; Britain, France and Russia on the other.

Here was a bonfire waiting for a match to start it off. The 'match' was the murder of an Austrian archduke by a Serbian nationalist. Austria attacked Serbia, Russia came to the aid of the Serbs (fellow-Slavs), Germany gathered its forces in fear of Russia. France refused to remain neutral, Germany attacked France, and Britain entered the war in France's support.

## The 'Great War'

Many people welcomed war. 'New' nations like Germany and Italy had the chance to prove their nationhood. Governments welcomed an event which turned their citizens' attention away from internal problems. Socialists believed war would hasten the victory of the working classes, as prophesied by Marx. Everyone thought the war would be fought in Europe and would soon be over. In fact, it lasted over four years and drew in Japan and the United States (on the Allies' side) and Turkey (on the German or Central Powers' side). The British dominions sent troops. Italy joined the Allies in the hope of gaining Austrian territory. The Balkan countries, the Arabs and other states became involved before the end.

The war in Europe soon became bogged down. The opposing sides faced each other from defensive trench systems in Belgium, northern France, Poland and Russia. The infantry was dominated by poison gas, machine guns and

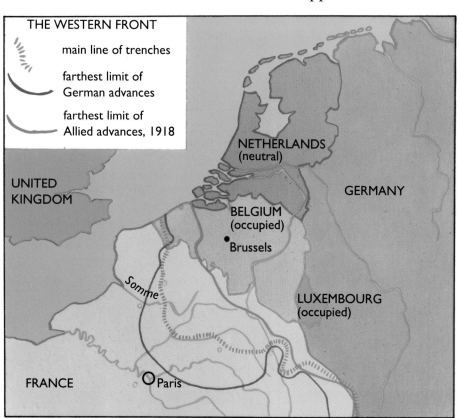

THE WESTERN FRONT

*(symbol)* main line of trenches

*(symbol)* farthest limit of German advances

*(symbol)* farthest limit of Allied advances, 1918

NETHERLANDS (neutral)

UNITED KINGDOM

GERMANY

BELGIUM (occupied)

Brussels

Somme

LUXEMBOURG (occupied)

FRANCE

Paris

*Probably the most effective weapon of trench warfare was not heavy artillery, poison gas, nor the tank (a very new weapon and little used), but the machine gun. Leaving the trenches to advance across open ground, soldiers were mown down in hundreds.*

artillery, and the battlefields became vast, muddy killing grounds. Casualties were horrifying. Nearly 1 million men died in a single battle (the Somme, 1916).

Fighting elsewhere was on a smaller scale. The British and German navies fought only one large naval battle (Jutland, 1916), with no clear result. German submarine attacks against civilian ships brought the United States into the war in 1917. After the failure of a large attack into France in 1918, Germany surrendered.

The costs of the war were huge. About 15 million people had been killed. The economy of Europe was in ruins. The only 'victor' was the United States, which came out of the war as the most powerful country in the world.

The war had other results. Many women had taken over absent soldiers' jobs; the movement for equality was strengthened. Under the pressure of war, the old empires of Austria and Turkey had collapsed. Russia ended the war with a Communist government, but elsewhere revolutionaries were disappointed, for the war had not produced victory for the working class. It had shown that nationalism, or patriotism, was stronger than the international brotherhood of workers.

## ARABS AND TURKS

With British support, the Arabs in the Near East rebelled against their Turkish rulers in 1916. The Turks were finally crushed at Megiddo (1918) and their empire divided up. In the peace treaty (1919) the Arab leaders did not gain all that had been promised to them, and the British and French remained dominant in the Middle East. Turkey became involved in war with Greece in 1920–22. The most successful Turkish general, later known as Ataturk (1881–1938), restored national pride and founded the modern republic of Turkey with himself as president (1923).

*Left: The first battles between aircraft took place in the First World War.*

# Russian Revolution

The effects of war also destroyed another old empire, that of Russia. Marx had expected the revolution of the working class to begin in an advanced industrial country such as Germany. Some revolutionary outbreaks did occur in Germany in 1918, but the one country where revolution was successful was the most backward – Russia. The Russian Revolution ended in the dominance of the Communist Party, which imposed rigid rules enforced by the secret police, and kept the Russian people prisoners in their own country for the next 70 years.

*Lenin was a refugee in Switzerland when the Russian Revolution broke out in 1917. He returned at once, assisted by the Germans who hoped he would cause trouble in Russia, then still at war with Germany.*

## Reform

Under Tsar Alexander II (reigned 1855–81) Russia advanced towards a more liberal society, but after he was assassinated, social progress stopped. Industrial progress continued, however, and Russia was faced with the extra problems of an industrializing society. Defeat in the Japanese war helped to set off a rebellion in 1905. It was defeated by force and the promise of reforms, but the reforms had little effect. In particular, the question of land ownership, of such importance to the peasants, was not solved. The warnings of a wise minister, Count Sergei Witte (1849–1915), were ignored.

## The Bolsheviks

War is often the cause of social changes, and another Russian failure in war, like that of 1905, provoked the revolution of 1917. Strikes and riots began in St Petersburg in March 1917. A workers' soviet, or governing council, was set up, and Tsar Nicholas II was forced to abdicate (he was later

*The decisive act in the October Revolution of 1917 was the Bolshevik takeover of the Winter Palace, the headquarters of the government, in Petrograd (previously St Petersburg, later Leningrad).*

murdered with all his family). The new provisional government, made up of socialists and liberals, was incapable. It tried to press on with the war, although the Russian army was fast breaking up. In November (October according to the calendar then in use in Russia), Lenin and the Bolsheviks (Communists) seized power. Their popular support was small, but they were far more determined than their opponents. They swiftly ended the war, at the price of handing over large territories to Germany. Then they concentrated on defeating their opponents inside Russia, who in 1918 received assistance from the British, French and others. Trotsky, Lenin's close associate, reorganized what became known as the 'Red' Army (red being the symbol of Communism), and the counter-revolutionaries, or 'White' Russians, were gradually suppressed.

The Bolsheviks expected the revolution to spread, and allowed Russian-controlled countries like Finland to become independent, thinking Communism would succeed there, too. It did not. The new Soviet government had many friends in other countries, but not among governments.

In order to keep control of Russia, the Bolsheviks used the same dictatorial methods as the government of the tsars, but they were more efficient and more ruthless.

After Lenin's death, Stalin became the Communist leader.

He reinforced the power of the Communist party, which became the supreme authority in the land in politics, law, even religion (the Communists attempted to destroy the Russian Orthodox Church). Opponents were treated as traitors. They were arrested and sent to prison, exile or death – with or without a trial.

*Stalin (above right) set out to make Communist Russia an industrial giant to rival the United States. Industrial development proceeded very rapidly, but at great cost.*

# Depression

A popular description of the First World War was that it was 'the war to end wars'. People who had lived through it certainly hoped never to fight another one. In fact, the First World War left Europe in a less stable condition than it had been in 1914, and created new problems as well. The peacemakers, who met at Versailles in 1919, had high hopes that the creation of a League of Nations would solve future international quarrels in a peaceful way. In fact, the Versailles treaty made a future war not less but more likely.

*Above right: A transatlantic liner. Rich people enjoyed a luxurious life style in the 1920s, the age of jazz, nightclubs, lavish parties and ocean cruises.*

### Europe after the war

The Bolsheviks were not alone in expecting international revolution. To prevent revolution was one of the tasks of the peacemakers in 1919. They agreed that national boundaries in Europe should be decided by the vote of the people. A number of new, or newly independent states emerged, including Poland, Czechoslovakia, Hungary and Yugoslavia. But in much of Europe the situation was too complicated to be arranged in a neat pattern of nations. Czechoslovakia, for instance, contained people of six other nationalities besides Czechs and Slovaks.

The peacemakers (the winners) blamed Germany for the war, and imposed harsh terms, including payment of huge sums of money as 'reparations' (compensation). Most Germans did not believe they were to blame, and felt betrayed by their new republican government, which had agreed on the terms of the peace. Others were also dissatisfied, notably Italy, which had not gained the territory it wanted. The United States, which had entered the war with decisive effect, went back to its old policy of keeping out of European affairs. It did not even become a member of the League of Nations, although the US president, Woodrow Wilson, had been the chief creator of the League. Germany and the Soviet Union (Russia) were not members, either.

*German children scavenging for food in 1921, when inflation made German money worthless.*

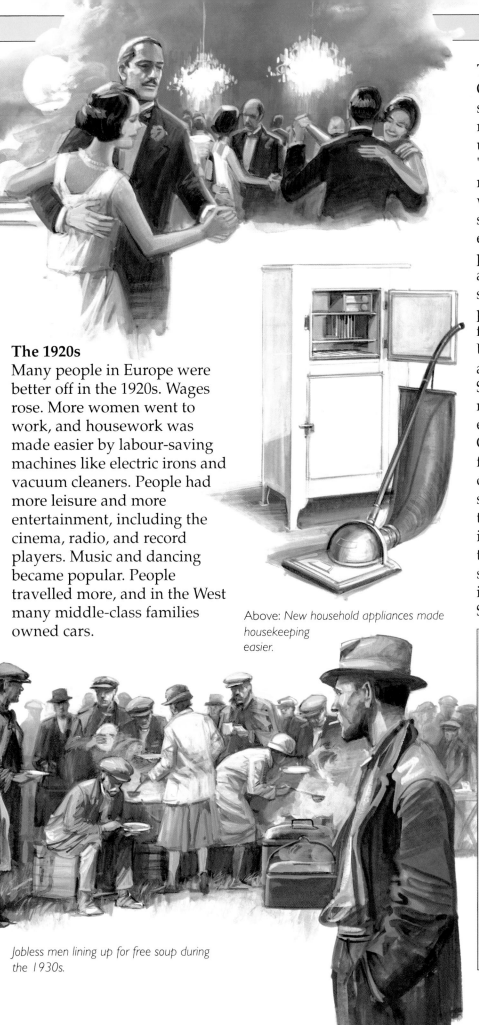

## The Great Depression

One drawback of the capitalist system is that, for no obvious reason, it produces economic ups and downs, or 'booms' and 'slumps'. The worst slump of modern times began in 1929 with a sudden disastrous fall in share prices on the US stock exchange. In three years, US production fell by half, and for a time the whole banking system seemed to be on the point of collapse. Thousands of firms went bankrupt. Unemployment shot up to about 15 million in the United States and roughly the same number in Europe as the economic depression spread. Communists gleefully looked forward to the collapse of the capitalist system. However, the system survived. Gradually, the economic situation improved, and the last traces of the Great Depression were swept away by the boost to industry provided by the Second World War.

## The 1920s

Many people in Europe were better off in the 1920s. Wages rose. More women went to work, and housework was made easier by labour-saving machines like electric irons and vacuum cleaners. People had more leisure and more entertainment, including the cinema, radio, and record players. Music and dancing became popular. People travelled more, and in the West many middle-class families owned cars.

Above: *New household appliances made housekeeping easier.*

*Jobless men lining up for free soup during the 1930s.*

### THE FAR EAST

Japan was already a world power by 1914. Its economic progress continued at a great rate until 1929, with Japanese goods replacing European ones in Asian markets. China, in spite of its revolution of 1911, was still economically backward, but the tide of nationalism was rising there too. Japan's aggressive imperialism led to the conquest of Manchuria from China in 1931. A full-scale invasion of China began in 1937, and the Nationalists were as eager to defeat the Communists as they were to defeat the Japanese. The war between China and Japan, however, soon became part of a larger one, the Second World War.

# New Dictators

The First World War signalled a breakdown in European civilization. The 20 years that followed were dominated by the rivalry of two ideologies, Communism and Fascism. Although directly hostile to each other, they shared many unpleasant characteristics. One was a belief in the total power of the state, supported by secret police and persecution of opponents. Both creeds showed a disregard for human rights, the absence of moral (or religious) principles and a brutal love of power. Law and justice counted for little. Power, especially military power, was all that mattered to the new dictators.

*In 1922, armed Fascist groups marched on Rome from Naples. The authorities did little to stop them and the government resigned. Mussolini (above) was then given the task of forming a government.*

## Fascism

Italy had suffered in the war, was disappointed by the peace, and endured severe economic difficulties afterwards. Most Italians were Roman Catholics and therefore hostile to Communism, which was ferociously anti-religious. But Italians, like many others, were dissatisfied with the 'failures' of liberal, parliamentary democracy. They were attracted by the Fascist party of Mussolini, who became prime minister in 1922. Democracy was quickly swept away and Mussolini, calling himself *Il Duce* ('the leader'), became a dictator. He began an adventurous foreign policy, conquering Ethiopia (an act which showed the League of Nations powerless to prevent aggression) and forming the Rome–Berlin Axis, an alliance with his fellow Fascist dictator, Hitler.

Germans were also bitter. They resented the terms of the Versailles treaty and scorned the weak parliamentary government of Weimar, which was unable to solve the economic crisis of the 1930s. Enough voters backed the National Socialist (Nazi) party to bring Hitler to power in 1933. The Nazis rapidly abolished all liberal and democratic institutions and established a barbaric totalitarian state. Riot and murder became part of government policy. A vicious campaign was waged against German Jews and others such as Gypsies, who were considered an inferior 'race'.

Attacks on liberal democracy from both Left (Communists) and Right (Fascists) also took place in other countries. Even France and Britain had Communist and Fascist parties, which caused civil disorder. Other countries, in central and southern Europe and in South America, came under dictatorial, fascist governments, which banished the rights of the individual in favour of the rights of the all-powerful state. In Spain, the clash between Left and Right produced a civil war (1936–39). The Fascists, aided by Mussolini and Hitler, were victorious and the Fascist general, Francisco Franco, became dictator (1939–75).

None of these governments, for all their brutality and crude ignorance, descended to the depths of Nazi Germany, and none murdered their own people in tens of thousands, as Stalin did in Russia.

*A Nazi rally. Hitler used these rallies to inflame people against Communists, capitalists, Jews and other objects of Nazi hatred (he would have found television very useful). In spite of the huge crowds, most Germans were not Nazis. They allowed Hitler to seize power partly through their own lack of interest in politics. Once in control, Hitler could not be removed.*

*Italian and German pilots practised bombing in the Spanish Civil War. Inset: Franco.*

## JAPAN

In Japan after 1929, people began to believe that economic difficulties could be solved by foreign conquests. Parliamentary government was unpopular and army officers, in particular, were infected with Fascist ideas. The government proved powerless against the rising tide of militarism. Many leading statesmen were murdered by right-wing terrorists. In 1936 Japan made an alliance with Nazi Germany and Fascist Italy against international Communism. The Japanese attacked China in 1937 and, with the outbreak of the Second World War, they seized the chance to create a Japanese empire in south-east Asia.

# The Second World War

The aggressive acts of Nazi Germany and the failure of the democratic powers, Britain and France (the 'policemen of Europe'), to stop them resulted in the Second World War (1939–45). This was truly a world war, fought in all continents. It was the first war in which air power played a decisive part and, as a result, civilian casualties were high. As in all wars, horrible things were done by all sides, but the special viciousness of German and Japanese conduct made it easy for their enemies to feel they were fighting in a just cause.

## Munich

The 1930s were marked by a series of crises created by illegal acts of aggression by Germany. In 1936 German troops marched into the Rhineland, which the Treaty of Versailles had made a non-military region. In 1938 the Nazis took over Austria. At the same time Hitler was uttering threats against Czechoslovakia, complaining that Germans living there were persecuted by the Czechs. In an attempt to prevent a German attack on Czechoslovakia, the prime ministers of Britain and France, plus Mussolini, met Hitler at Munich in Germany (1938). They agreed to hand over the Sudetenland, the part of Czechoslovakia most heavily populated by Germans. The Czech government was not consulted. Six months later Hitler took over the rest of Czechoslovakia.

Hitler also considered part of Poland to be rightfully German, and after inventing a quarrel, he ordered his armies to invade Poland in September 1939. He expected Britain and France to hold back, as they had at Munich. But this time Britain and France, Poland's allies, declared war.

## Main campaigns

Poland was beyond help, and within a year the Germans had also conquered Norway, Denmark, Belgium, Holland and finally France herself. Italy entered the war on the German side. However, Hitler was unable to defeat Britain. To invade, the Germans needed to win control of the air, and in the Battle of Britain (1940) they failed to destroy British air power.

The Germans unwisely attacked Russia in 1941 (despite having signed a defensive agreement with Stalin in 1939). In December,

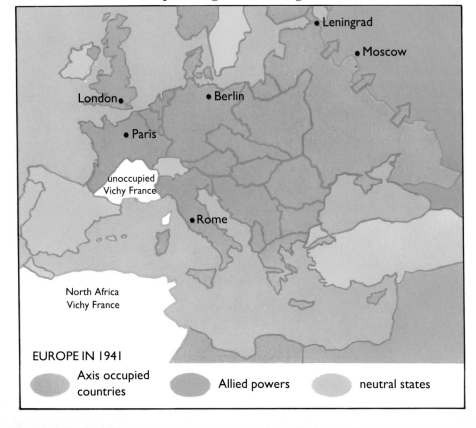

EUROPE IN 1941

Axis occupied countries

Allied powers

neutral states

London•

• Berlin

• Paris

unoccupied Vichy France

•Rome

• Leningrad

• Moscow

North Africa Vichy France

Above: *The Japanese attack on Pearl Harbor destroyed several battleships, but no aircraft carriers, which were the most powerful weapons in the sea battles of the Pacific campaign.*

By 1943 the final result was in no doubt. The Germans were defeated in North Africa and in Russia, at Stalingrad, where a whole German army surrendered. Italy withdrew from the war, and Mussolini was murdered. British, US and other Allied forces fought their way into Germany, while the Russians advanced from the east. In May 1945 Hitler admitted defeat by killing himself. The Japanese refused to surrender until the Americans dropped atomic bombs on the cities of Hiroshima and Nagasaki.

The war had destroyed the Nazi tyranny, which had caused the deaths of millions in concentration camps. The war had also destroyed the military ambitions of Japan. But large parts of Europe were in ruins, and Europe had ceased to be the centre of world power. Across the battlefields, the two victorious 'superpowers' – the Soviet Union and the United States – confronted each other.

the Japanese launched a surprise air attack on the US naval base of Pearl Harbor, Hawaii, bringing the United States into the war.

Major campaigns were fought in North Africa, in the Atlantic (where German submarines attacked ships bringing supplies to Britain from America), in south-east Asia (which had been quickly overrun by the Japanese) and in the Pacific (where aircraft carriers proved the key naval weapon). Fighting on a smaller scale took place in many other parts of the world, including German-occupied countries where underground resistance fighters showed amazing courage.

Below: *German cities such as Dresden and Hamburg were almost completely destroyed by massive US and British bombing raids. German civilians probably suffered more than others, but there was little sympathy for them in Allied countries.*

# References

**Allies**  A name given to countries bound to aid each other in war; in particular, the 'Western' allies (Britain, France, the United States and others) in the world wars.

**Anti-Semitism**  Hostility towards Jews, a feature of Christianity throughout history, which seemed to have faded away until it was revived in the 19th century and reached a peak in Nazi Germany.

**Appeasement**  The policy of trying to settle the demands of an aggressive power by peaceful methods and concessions, adopted by Britain and France towards Germany in the 1930s.

**Axis Powers**  Germany, Austria and their Second World War allies.

**Balkan Wars**  Two wars between the Balkan countries of south-east Europe in 1912–13, resulting from rival territorial ambitions among these former Turkish provinces.

**Bolsheviks**  Russian revolutionaries, originally the extreme Left wing of the Russian Socialist party, led by Lenin; their name means 'the majority', but they weren't.

**Chiang Kai-shek** (1886–1975) Chinese statesman, leader of the Kuomintang (from 1925) and president of the Chinese Nationalist government in the 1930s and 1940s.

**Churchill, Winston** (1874–1965) British prime minister, 1940–45, an inspiring wartime leader.

**Comintern**  'Communist International', an organization founded by Lenin in 1915 to aid workers in all countries; it became an instrument of Soviet foreign policy, controlling Communist parties in other countries.

**Commonwealth** (originally 'British Commonwealth')  The former British empire, countries that were, or are, ruled by Britain.

**Dardanelles campaign**  An Allied expedition against the Turks in 1915, intended to capture Constantinople; it failed and the troops withdrew in 1916.

**De Gaulle, Charles** (1890–1970) French general, leader of the Free French forces in exile in Britain 1940–44, president of France 1944–46 and 1958–69.

**Fascism**  A political movement in Italy, anti-democratic, nationalistic, militaristic; the name is given to other extreme-Right groups like the Nazis in Germany.

**'Great Purge'**  An episode in the Soviet Union, 1936–38, when tens of thousands of Soviet citizens were executed or exiled to Siberia.

**Hitler, Adolf** (1889–1945)  German Nazi leader (*führer*), 1933–1945, who wrote *Mein Kampf* ('My Struggle', 1927) revealing his political views, including fanatical anti-Semitism, was elected chancellor, destroyed democratic institutions and created a totalitarian state; his aggressive foreign policy led to war in 1939.

**Kuomintang**  Chinese Nationalist party, which formed the government in the 1930s though fighting a civil war with Communists (who won in 1949).

**League of Nations**  The international organization founded in 1919 to settle international conflicts, replaced by the United Nations in 1946.

**Lenin**  (real name Vladimir Ulyanov, 1870–1924)  Russian revolutionary, Bolshevik leader; as prime minister (in effect dictator) he reorganized Russia as a Marxist (Communist) state.

**Mandate**  An 'Order', by the League of Nations, giving authority to one country to govern another, especially former provinces of Turkey mandated to Britain, France or other states in 1919.

**Mensheviks**  The less violent revolutionaries of the Russian Socialist party; *see* **Bolsheviks**

**Mussolini, Benito** (1883–1945) Italian fascist leader, who created the Fascist party (1919), creating disturbances in Italy; appointed prime minister in 1922 he made himself a dictator, known as *Il Duce* ('the leader').

**New Deal**  The policy of President Roosevelt's government to rescue the United States from the Depression of the 1930s by huge programmes of government spending and social welfare.

**Palestine Mandate**  The British government of Palestine, 1920–48.

**Roosevelt, Franklin D.** (1882–1945) US president, 1933–45, who fought the Depression with his New Deal programme, aided Britain against Germany from 1939 and brought the United States into the war in 1941; with Churchill and Stalin, he was the chief Allied war leader.

**Stalin, Joseph** (real name Dzhugashvili, 1879–1953) Communist leader of the Soviet Union from 1924, carried out rapid industrialization, enforced the power of the Communist party and himself by ruthless policies (*see* **'Great Purge'**), directed the Russian war effort and secured a ring of subservient 'satellite' states around Russian frontiers after 1945.

**Suffragettes**  The militant wing of the British women's movement demanding female suffrage (votes for women).

**Totalitarianism**  The control by government of every activity of its citizens, including literature, art and religion.

**Trotsky, Leon** (real name Lev Bronstein, 1879–1940)  Bolshevik revolutionary and close associate of Lenin, who organized the Red Army after 1917, fell out with Stalin and went into exile.

**Versailles, Treaty of**  The peace settlement of 1919, imposing harsh terms on the Germans, who signed it under protest.

**Vichy**  French town, capital of the region of France not occupied by German troops, 1940–44, though under German control.

**Weimar Republic**  The democratic, republican government of Germany 1919–33 (its constitution was agreed at the town of Weimar).

# The Electronic Age

# Rise and Fall of Empires

After 1945, the leading countries of Europe – France, Germany, Italy – were no longer 'great powers'. Britain still seemed to be a great power, but that was the result of the major part it had played in the war. Its political and economic power was in reality much smaller. The recovery of Western Europe depended on help from the United States, especially through the Marshall Plan. Eastern Europe was dominated by the Soviet Union, divided from the West by what Churchill called an 'Iron Curtain'. While the Soviet Union created a Communist empire in Europe after the war, the old imperial powers rapidly surrendered their own overseas empires. As a result, within 20 years, the number of independent states in the world doubled.

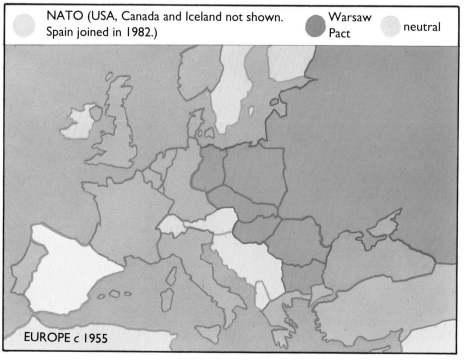

NATO (USA, Canada and Iceland not shown. Spain joined in 1982.)  Warsaw Pact  neutral

EUROPE c 1955

Above: *The civil war between Nationalists and Communists in China ended with the success of the Communists in 1949. The Nationalists continued to hold Taiwan. Mao Tse-tung, the Communist leader, became a kind of Chinese Stalin, imposing dictatorial rule and allowing no opposition.*

## Asia

Even the British government had long recognized that India should become independent. The Indian Congress Party, following Gandhi's policy of 'passive resistance', was the leader of Hindu nationalism, and by 1945 the British government was eager to cooperate.

Disagreement between Hindus and Muslims, however, resulted in the creation of a separate Muslim state of Pakistan when in 1947 independence came amid widespread Hindu–Muslim riots. In 1971 East Pakistan, aided by her neighbour, India, broke away to become the separate state of Bangladesh.

Farther east, Indonesia, formerly a Dutch colony, declared independence in 1945. The Federation of Malaysia was created (1963) after a guerilla war against the Communist rebels.

Worse violence affected south-east Asia. The French were driven out of Indo-China in the 1950s, but the whole region became a battlefield between the forces of Communism and democracy. Major wars were fought in Korea (1950–53) and Vietnam (1962–75) where the large US forces engaged against Communist-backed North Vietnam were finally forced to withdraw (1973) – the first American defeat in war.

1976. A long civil war between the French and Algerian nationalists ended when Algeria gained independence in June 1962. Civil wars in Zaire (formerly the Belgian Congo) and Nigeria resulted from the efforts of provinces to break away on their own. Zimbabwe (formerly Rhodesia) was ruled by a white minority government from 1965, when the government declared its independence from Britain, until 1979, when it accepted democratic rule. South Africa was a special case. Its white population was large, and the dominant Afrikaners had been settled in the country since the 17th century. The racial policy known as *apartheid* ('separateness') was adopted in 1948, excluding non-whites from citizenship and reserving the government, wealth and resources of the country for whites.

Above: *The British flag is lowered as a former colony becomes independent. Some colonies gained independence without serious violence, but faced severe problems later. Europeans had drawn the boundaries of colonies without considering national or tribal divisions, and this caused social conflicts and civil war in many African countries.*

Below: *After a short civil war, the Right-wing dictator of Cuba, Fulgencio Batista, was overthrown by rebels led by Fidel Castro in 1958. Once in power, Castro became a firm ally of the Soviet Union, heading the only Communist state in the Americas.*

## African nationalism

The many European colonies in Africa became independent states almost as fast as they had become colonies during the imperial 'scramble' for Africa in the late 19th century. In many of these new countries, the process was peaceful, even friendly, and the independent states kept some links with their former rulers (such as membership of the Commonwealth). However, there were violent exceptions, especially in countries with a large European settler population. Portuguese Angola and Mozambique had to wait for independence until the overthrow of the military dictatorship in Portugal in

# United Nations

The atomic bombs dropped on Japan in 1945, and the more powerful nuclear weapons developed in the 1950s, made the prospect of war more terrifying. Wars have been as frequent in the last half of the 20th century as in any previous age, but they have been 'local' wars, fought in a small region, without nuclear weapons. At times a third world war looked likely, but did not happen. The United Nations has had no more success than the League of Nations in preventing violence. But it has at least provided a world assembly where international problems can be discussed. Many other organizations have worked for closer international cooperation in smaller regions.

**The UN and the Cold War**
From the beginning, all nations were equally represented in the UN General Assembly, but the Security Council (concerned with peace and security) had five permanent members plus ten others elected for two years each, by region. In its early years, the UN was dominated by the superpowers. Their permanent membership of the Security Council gave them the power to veto (forbid) any UN policy they disliked. As more countries gained independence and became members, the balance of power changed slightly. Nevertheless, as long as the Cold War – superpower hostility without actual fighting – continued, decisive action by the UN in an international crisis proved almost impossible.

The Cold War produced a series of international crises, any of which might have resulted in world war but for the universal fear of nuclear weapons. In 1948 the Soviet Union blockaded West Berlin which, though in East (Communist) Germany, belonged to the West. The West (Britain, France and the United States) flew in supplies by air. The Russians did not interfere and eventually lifted the blockade. To prevent East Germans escaping to the West, a wall was built across Berlin.

A shooting war was provoked by Communist North Korea's invasion of democratic South Korea in 1950. A UN force (chiefly US) repelled the invasion, which was backed by Communist China. In 1962, the United States discovered Soviet nuclear missiles in Cuba. The US government demanded their removal, and after a few days, when war seemed certain, the Soviets agreed.

Besides political debates, the UN set up agencies like the World Health Organization, the Food and Agriculture Organization, and UNICEF (children's aid).

Right: The task of UNWRA was to look after refugees, like the 'boat people' who fled from Vietnam after the Communist victory in 1975. The huge number of people who became refugees through political or other causes presented a world problem that was often too large for the resources made available.

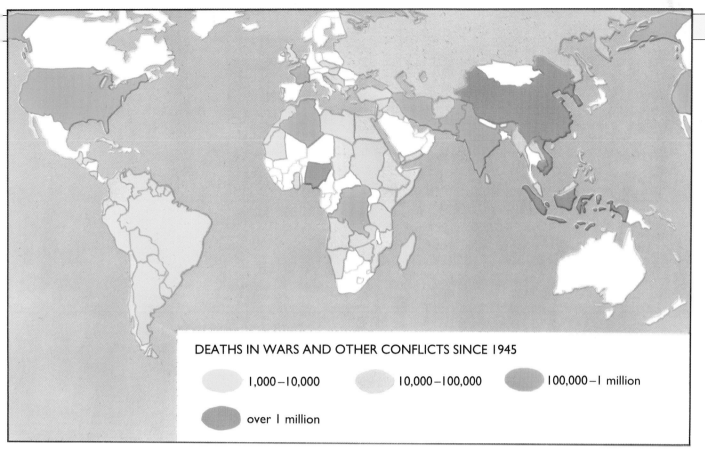

### DEATHS IN WARS AND OTHER CONFLICTS SINCE 1945

- 1,000–10,000
- 10,000–100,000
- 100,000–1 million
- over 1 million

*Deaths in local wars and civil conflicts between 1945 and 1985 were greater than military casualties in the Second World War.*

## The superpowers

Each of the superpowers had its own problems. Not all the Communist states of Europe obeyed Soviet orders. Yugoslavia and Albania became independent; Romania followed its own foreign policy; there were riots in Poland and East Germany, and serious rebellions in Hungary (1956), Czechoslovakia (1968) (both crushed by Soviet tanks) and Poland (1981). A more serious problem was the economic failure of the Communist system compared with the democratic, capitalist system of the West. By the 1970s the Soviet Union's military power was greater than that of the United States, but the living standards of its people were far lower.

Unlike the Soviet Union, the United States had allies, rather than satellites, and disagreements were common. France, in particular, often followed foreign policies different from those of the United States. For the United States, the gravest internal problem concerned the civil rights of black Americans. In the 1960s new laws were passed to enforce equal treatment for blacks and whites. But poverty among blacks could not be easily cured. Heavy casualties, and final defeat in the Vietnam War showed that the US was not invincible, and shook the American people's confidence in their nation.

# Third World

The countries of the world, nearly all of them represented in the UN, fell roughly into three groups or blocs: the Communist bloc, dominated by the Soviet Union; the Western bloc, led by the United States, and a third group, sometimes called the Third World, made up of countries in Africa, Asia and Latin America. Although a few of these countries had valuable natural resources, the Third World countries were generally under-developed and poor, compared with the West. Western countries grew richer between 1950 and 1990, but most Third World countries did not.

## Rich and poor

In some ways, the great rise in wealth in Western countries (including Australia, New Zealand and, most of all, Japan) during the second half of the 20th century was gained at the expense of the Third World. Western countries were mainly manufacturers. Third World countries were producers of food and raw materials. While the price of manufactured goods rose steadily, the price of raw materials did not. The Third World countries, short of money, had to pay more for the manufactures they needed, while the industrialized countries paid less for their raw materials.

In 1973 the countries belonging to OPEC – the main producers of oil – raised the price of oil by about 400 per cent. This did not help non-oil producers. Attempts by other producer-nations to follow this example had little success.

The gap between rich and poor existed not only between different countries but also among the citizens of the same country. Some Latin American countries, for example, contained a small number of very rich people, but also overcrowded and filthy slums where millions of people lived in abject poverty.

## Foreign aid

Economic aid from the rich nations to the poor nations took many forms, but the most important was in the form of money for industrial development, usually in the form of loans at low interest rates. Loan programmes were

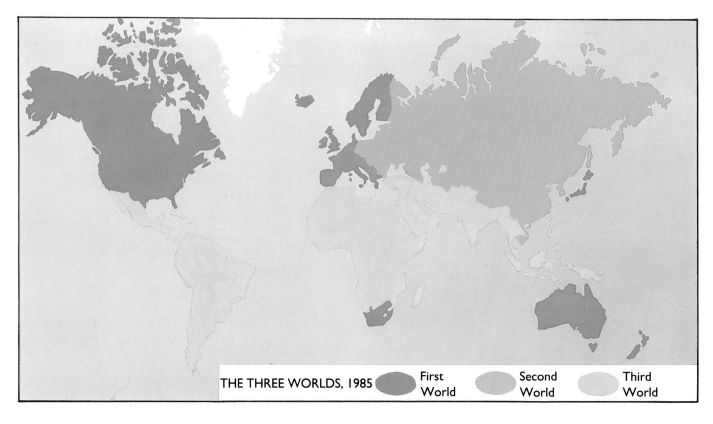

THE THREE WORLDS, 1985    First World    Second World    Third World

*Famine has not been conquered in Third World countries. A change in climate causing the Sahara desert to spread farther south brought starvation to millions in Africa.*

arranged through the World Bank, a United Nations organization. Foreign aid did not solve fundamental problems; sometimes aid was directed to the wrong purposes, and sometimes developing countries could not repay huge debts.

The difficulties of Third World countries were political and social, as well as economic.

Some countries suffered at times from bad government. Most had to deal with fast-growing populations, lack of education, and old-fashioned farming methods. A typical developing country might increase its production of food by (for example) five per cent in a year. But if the population increased by six per cent, it was worse off than before.

## WORLD HEALTH

The number of babies out of every 1,000 born in 1983 who died before their first birthday (sample regions). Figures in brackets indicate the number of people to each doctor.

**Less than 20:** North America (550), Europe (400-600), Australia and New Zealand (600), Japan (750).

**20-40:** Soviet Union (250), Argentina (420), Venezuela (950), China (780).

**40-60:** Mexico (1,250), Colombia (1,700), Thailand (6,850), Mongolia (450).

**60-100:** Brazil (1,150), Peru (1,480), Ecuador (1,500), South Africa (2,000), Kenya (10,000), Libya (750), Indonesia (11,700).

**Over 100:** Most of Africa (7,000 in Ghana, 15,000 in Angola, 72,000 in Ethiopia), India (2,700), Pakistan (2,900), Bangladesh (7,200), Iran (2,300), Bolivia (2,100).

## LIFE EXPECTANCY

The age to which a man could expect to live in the 1980s (sample countries). Women lived slightly longer.

Japan 74, France 71, USA 70, Soviet Union 66, China 66, Nicaragua 59, Libya 56, India 53, Tanzania 49, Bolivia 49, Afghanistan 37.

## EDUCATION

The number of people in every 100 who could not read and write in 1983 (sample countries).

USA, Canada, Soviet Union, most of Europe: less than 1.

Brazil, China: over 20.

India, Iran, Algeria, Egypt: over 40.

Niger, Bangladesh, Pakistan: over 60.

*Left: In many Third World cities, there is a startling contrast between the way of life of the rich and, a street or two away, the most horrible slums where people scavenge for food in rubbish heaps to stay alive.*

# Oil and the Middle East

After the Second World War the world became increasingly dependent on oil to provide energy for industry and transport. The richest oil reserves were in parts of the Middle East, and the Middle East was one of the most unstable and violent regions of the world. Oil itself was one reason for conflict. More important were the existence of the Jewish state of Israel, the ambitions of Arab nationalism, and a militant form of Islam.

## Israel

Jews began migrating to British-ruled Palestine in growing numbers in the 1920s, against local Arab opposition. Their numbers increased after 1945, and in 1947 the UN divided Palestine into Jewish and Arab provinces. Arab nations refused to accept this division. In 1948, under attack from the Arabs, the state of Israel (much larger than the UN province) was founded. The Jewish ambition for their own state was understood in most countries, because of the Jews' sufferings under the Nazis. But it was fiercely opposed by the Arabs, especially the Palestinians, about a million of whom became refugees in the Lebanon and other Arab countries. With support from the United States, Israel prospered. The Arabs were defeated in two further wars (1967 and 1973), while the Middle East became a battleground of the Cold War.

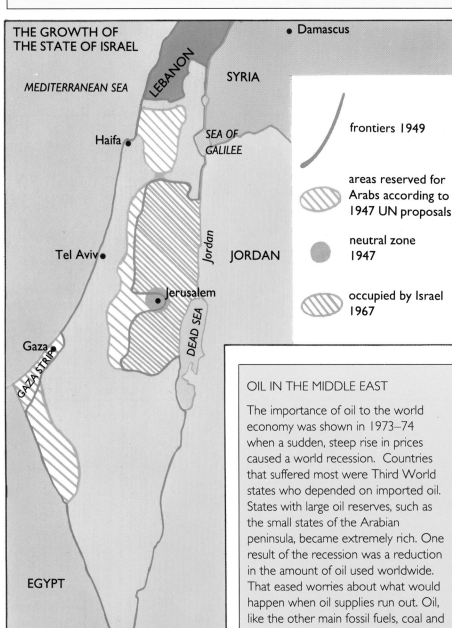

THE GROWTH OF THE STATE OF ISRAEL

Damascus

MEDITERRANEAN SEA

LEBANON

SYRIA

Haifa

SEA OF GALILEE

Tel Aviv

Jordan

JORDAN

Jerusalem

DEAD SEA

Gaza

GAZA STRIP

EGYPT

Eilat • Aqaba

SAUDI ARABIA

frontiers 1949

areas reserved for Arabs according to 1947 UN proposals

neutral zone 1947

occupied by Israel 1967

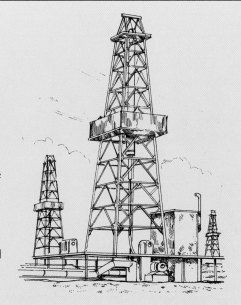

## OIL IN THE MIDDLE EAST

The importance of oil to the world economy was shown in 1973–74 when a sudden, steep rise in prices caused a world recession. Countries that suffered most were Third World states who depended on imported oil. States with large oil reserves, such as the small states of the Arabian peninsula, became extremely rich. One result of the recession was a reduction in the amount of oil used worldwide. That eased worries about what would happen when oil supplies run out. Oil, like the other main fossil fuels, coal and gas, is a 'non-renewable resource': the oil fields will not last for ever.

## The Arab Nations

Failure in war against Israel encouraged revolt against old-style Arab rulers. Gamel Abdel Nasser (1918–70), seized power in Egypt in the 1950s. He became the leader of Arab nationalism, hostile to the West and supported by the Soviet Union. When Nasser nationalized the Suez Canal in 1956, British and French troops briefly invaded Suez but, without US support, were forced to withdraw.

Revolutionary forces were at work elsewhere in the region. An extreme government seized power in Syria in 1961. Militant Islamic regimes came to power in Libya in 1969 and Iran in 1979, overthrowing the old monarchies. These governments were intensely hostile to the West. They were suspected of supporting terrorist activities, such as bombings, hijacking airliners, and kidnappings, often carried out by extremist Palestinian groups (and, in other parts of the world, by extremist groups of many kinds). Revolutionary Arab regimes generally enforced totalitarian rule and sided with the Communist bloc, while traditional monarchies, like that of Saudi Arabia, sided with the West. All were united against Israel although Egypt, after Nasser's death, changed its policy and signed a peace agreement with Israel in 1978 (to the anger of other Arab states).

A boundary dispute between Iran and Iraq was the cause of the Iran–Iraq war (1980–88), which caused over a million casualties. The Iraqi dictator, Saddam Hussein, in another quarrel over boundaries, invaded and occupied the small (but oil-rich) sheikhdom of Kuwait in 1990. His forces were expelled in 1991 by a US-led force with the support of the UN.

*The dwindling supply of fossil fuels and the loss of confidence in nuclear power encouraged experiments in using the forces of nature (sun, ocean tides, winds) to generate electric power. This 'wind farm' in California, USA, supplied a whole town with electricity in the 1980s.*

### ACCIDENT AT CHERNOBYL

From the 1950s, many governments saw nuclear power as an answer to future fuel shortages. By the 1990s these hopes had faded. Nuclear power stations had proved more expensive to build and operate than expected. Also, the process of nuclear fission, which produces the power, is highly dangerous, chiefly due to the harmful radiation given off. The explosion of a nuclear power plant at Chernobyl in the Soviet Union in 1986 was a grim warning. Radiation effects from the accident reached Britain and Scandinavia.

# Communications

Ever since the voyages of discovery during the Renaissance, the world has seemed to be growing smaller. The travels of conquerors, merchants, colonists and others made people aware of different societies in distant lands. Advances in transport and communications speeded up this process: railways, motor vehicles and most recently aeroplanes made long-distance travel easier; telegraph, telephones, radio and television did the same for communications. Still more dramatic developments took place in communications in the last half of the 20th century, as a result of space exploration and computer technology.

### A smaller world

The amazing advances in communications, which would have seemed impossible to people living less than 100 years ago, made the world seem a smaller place. Through radio and television, news could be broadcast throughout the world in minutes. From the 1970s, communications satellites in orbit around the Earth were used to 'bounce' television and telephone signals around the curve of the planet. People anywhere on Earth could speak to each other by telephone and send documents almost anywhere instantly with telex and, by the 1980s, fax machines.

Quicker travel also brought distant communities closer. The railway tunnel under the English Channel makes it possible for people who work in London to live in France and vice versa.

Speedy communications and travel brought economic changes, too. Helped by the breaking down of national trade barriers, business became international. A European business person could fly to New York for a meeting and return the same day. However, personal travel became less necessary as improvements in communications allowed several people, each in a different continent, to 'meet' and do business by telephone and television contact.

Technology advanced rapidly in industry and other fields. Cars could be made by robots; businesses benefited from the use of computers, with their enormous powers of storing and retrieving information and performing calculations. The invention of the microprocessor in the 1970s made small computers common in offices, classrooms and homes.

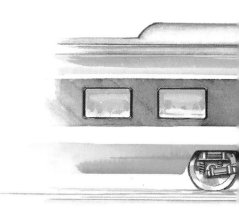

Above: *Communications satellites send signals around the Earth.*

Below: *The French High-Speed Train (TGV) travelled at up to 300 kph in the 1980s.*

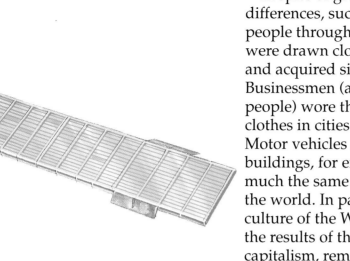

In spite of great cultural differences, such as language, people throughout the world were drawn closer together and acquired similar habits. Businessmen (and young people) wore the same sort of clothes in cities everywhere. Motor vehicles and office buildings, for example, looked much the same in any city in the world. In particular, the culture of the West, especially the results of the success of capitalism, remained a powerful influence throughout the world after the Western colonial empires had disappeared. People everywhere wanted to make economic progress and improve their standards of living. These ideas had hardly existed, even in the West, until the Industrial Revolution.

Above: *Common aids to communications in the 1990s: satellite TV receiver, 'fax' (facsimile) machine, computer.*

Below: *The most popular form of surface transport proved to be motor vehicles. By 1990 the United States had more than half as many cars as people. Hong Kong had one car for every 4m (13 ft) of road.*

### COMMUNICATIONS REVOLUTION

The use of space was the most dramatic example of the way scientific advances helped speed up communications in the late 20th century. The Russians were the first to launch a successful artificial space satellite in 1957. In 1961 Yuri Gagarin became the first space traveller by orbiting the Earth once in an hour and a half. The United States landed the first astronauts on the Moon in 1969 and in 1981 developed the space 'shuttle', the first craft capable of returning to the Earth and landing, like an aeroplane, ready for re-use. Unmanned spacecraft penetrated deep into outer space to explore the planets, and by the 1990s a large number of satellites were circling the Earth relaying TV signals, recording weather changes, and making scientific surveys of the planet.

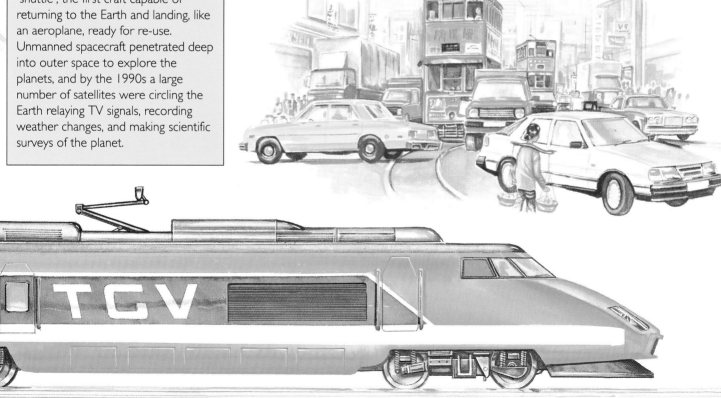

# A New View of the Earth

The history of the human race is the story of the conquest of nature by human beings. In the late 20th century, many people began to fear that their race had been *too* successful. Not only had human beings succeeded in conquering nature for their own purposes; they were in danger of destroying it. As they still depended on nature for the necessities of life, such as food to eat, water to drink and air to breathe, they were in danger of destroying themselves.

## Population

In 1930 the world contained about 2,000 million people. By 1990 it contained nearly three times as many. Experts believe that the population will go on increasing until about the 23rd century and, for some of that time, at an even faster rate. Most of this increase will take place in Third World countries. They already contain about three-quarters of the world's people, and they are also the countries where poverty is greatest.

Growing populations strained the resources of these countries, where living standards were already low. In some tropical countries, valuable forests were destroyed for farming land or fuel. In central Africa and other regions, fertile soil was ruined by the grazing of too many animals or by farming the land too heavily. In many countries, especially in South America, people who could not survive in the countryside came to the cities to live in crowded slums. Between about 1960 and 1990, the gap between the world's rich and poor grew even larger. Even those Third World countries which managed to increase their income did not increase it as fast as Western countries, where living standards rose very fast after about 1960.

Below: *Oil spills caused widespread local pollution of seas and coasts. The wreck of the oil tanker* Exxon Valdez *in 1989 spread oil over nearly 13,000 square kilometres (5,000 square miles) off the coast of Alaska, killing many forms of wildlife.*

## Pollution and resources

During the Cold War period, people feared the world might be destroyed by nuclear war. From about 1980 they had a greater fear that it would be destroyed by other causes. Natural resources, such as oil, would one day be used up. Changes in climate would cause farming failures and flooding. Changes in climate, as well as other dangers to the natural environment, were blamed on pollution, such as that caused by fuel-burning factories and engines. The future dangers predicted by scientists could not be proved, but in the 1980s some signs of them appeared. One example was the hole in the ozone layer (a thin section of the upper atmosphere that protects the Earth from harmful ultraviolet rays from the Sun). The cause of the hole was probably industrial pollution, which was also blamed for acid rain and the Earth-warming 'greenhouse effect'.

### THE EARTH AS A LIVING THING

As a result of the invention of spacecraft, people were able to learn many things about the Earth through various scientific observations carried out by satellites in orbit. Photographs of the Earth taken from space gave people a new view of the world. It was easier to understand that the Earth is a small and fragile object in the universe, and to see it as a single biological whole in which all forms of life exist in balance. It was also possible to see signs of damage to the environment, such as air pollution in heavily populated, industrial areas.

Among the harmful changes to the natural environment resulting from rising population and rising hopes for wealth was the steady destruction of the tropical rain forest by timber companies, miners, farmers and others. Once destroyed, rain forest will not grow again, and the land soon becomes useless for agriculture.

The worsening state of the environment concerned everyone, but different groups disagreed about what should be done to stop it. Poor countries were reluctant to preserve forests and other natural habitats at the cost of their own economic development. Industrial countries in Europe and North America were unwilling to reduce their own waste and pollution. Some steps towards international cooperation were taken at a conference on the environment held in Rio de Janeiro, Brazil, in 1992.

Below: *Some environmental groups employed militant methods of protest. In the 1980s members of Greenpeace tried to prevent Japanese ships catching whales.*

# End of the Cold War

From 1945 to 1989 world affairs were dominated by the Cold War – the rivalry between the Communist Soviet Union and the capitalist United States – each supported (willingly or not) by satellites and allies. China (also Communist but hostile to the Soviet Union) ought to have been a third superpower, but it was so badly governed under Mao Tse-tung and his successors, and suffered so much internal violence, that it played a small part in world affairs. Soviet–US relations varied; sometimes they were so hostile that a 'hot' war seemed likely; sometimes almost friendly. After Soviet leader Mikhail Gorbachev came to power in 1985, the Cold War came rapidly to an end.

Berliners chopped down portions of the Berlin Wall in November 1989. The wall had been built in 1961 to prevent East Germans escaping to freedom in West Berlin (West Germany).

## Wars and conflicts

The mighty weapons of the two 'superpowers', terrible enough to destroy the entire world, prevented direct war between them. However, small wars, rebellions and other forms of violence (such as terrorism) actually increased after the Second World War. There were nearly 100 wars between 1945 and 1990, almost all in Asia, Africa or South America. About 20 million people were killed, and an even larger number became refugees. In 1990 at least 15 million people were living as refugees in foreign countries. Many had no hope of ever returning home.

Most of these conflicts were between rival groups of people, not between nations, and most failed to solve the problems that caused them. In wars of that kind, the military strength of the superpowers had little effect. The United States was defeated in Vietnam; the Soviet Union was forced to give up its support for the Communist government in Afghanistan in 1989 after failing to defeat its opponents in nine years of war.

Some of the worst wars, however, were fought for the oldest reason: the desire of one nation or group to increase its land and power at the expense of another. Examples were the Chinese occupation of Tibet (from 1950), the Falklands War (1982) and the Iran–Iraq war (1980–88). Iraq also occupied Kuwait in 1990, but was expelled by an international force led by the United States.

*Modern weapons, supplied by industrialized countries, made even small, local conflicts more deadly.*

state of armed hostility with the United States – in effect, ending the Cold War.

Under Gorbachev the Russian people gained greater freedom, and Russia relaxed its grip on Eastern Europe. By 1990, Soviet-controlled satellite states such as Czechoslovakia, Hungary and Poland became independent democracies. To some extent their new governments gave up a socialist economic system in favour of the capitalist free market. East Germany was reunited with democratic West Germany. Other Communist regimes, such as the crude and savage Ceaucescu government in Romania, also fell. Inside the Soviet Union, the non-Russian republics also demanded independence. This nationalism resulted in the break-up of the Soviet Union and the end of an era in Europe which had begun with the Bolshevik Revolution of 1917.

Above: *As Russia relaxed its grip on Eastern Europe, individual republics and nations claimed independence.*

Below: *The dramatic change in the Soviet Union brought about by Gorbachev's policies of glasnost and perestroika ('reconstruction') promised better times for Europeans and the West. But neither Communism nor capitalism succeeded in reducing the enormous gap between rich and poor nations, which remained the world's biggest single human problem.*

## Glasnost

The action against Iraq was authorized by the UN. The Soviet Union gave passive (non-military) support to the United States and their allies – the first time that the two superpowers had voted in agreement in a big international crisis since 1945. The Cold War was over.

By the 1980s Communist rule was unpopular not only in the 'satellite' countries of Eastern Europe but also in the Soviet Union itself. People hated the lack of freedom – a person might be imprisoned simply for criticizing the government. Furthermore, Communist government had proved an economic failure. Living standards behind the Iron Curtain were far lower than in the West. In the Soviet Union, Gorbachev's policy of *glasnost* ('openness') was designed to save money by reducing military expenses. This was done by giving up some weapons and ending the

# References

**Acid rain** Rainfall containing dissolved gases, such as sulphur dioxide from coal-burning power stations, which killed trees and fish in lakes in some regions.

**African National Congress** A nationalist organization in South Africa, founded in 1912, which aimed for a non-racial society and organized opposition to apartheid; its most respected leader, Nelson Mandela, was released after 26 years in prison, in 1990.

**Birth control** Efforts to reduce the number of babies born, in various ways, in order to slow down the rise in population.

**Chernobyl** A town in the Ukraine where an accident in a nuclear power station occurred in 1986.

**Conservation** Caring for nature, including plants and animals in danger of extinction as well as the Earth as a whole living thing.

**Economic imperialism** A name given to the continuing economic dependence of ex-colonies in Africa and Asia on their former European rulers.

**Environment** The surroundings in which a living thing exists, including climate, effects of other living things, etc.

**Falklands War** A brief campaign (1982) by a British force to expel Argentinians who had occupied the Falkland Islands (Malvinas), a British colony.

**Fossil fuels** Fuels such as oil, coal and natural gas, which formed many millions of years ago from the remains of plants; their drawbacks are that (1) they cause pollution and environmental damage, and (2) the supply is limited and will one day run out.

**Gandhi, Mohandas** (1869–1948) Indian nationalist leader known as Mahatma ('Great Spirit'), leader of the struggle for independence from Britain by a policy of peaceful non-cooperation, who became a greatly respected international figure.

**Gorbachev, Mikhail** (born 1931) Head of the Soviet Communist party (from 1985) and Soviet president (1989–1991), who introduced the liberal policies of *glasnost* and *perestroika*.

**'Green'** In politics, a description of parties, groups or individuals whose chief concern is the health of the environment.

**Greenhouse effect** A warming of the Earth caused by industrial gases in the atmosphere that prevent heat escaping into space; future effects may include a rise in sea levels causing huge floods.

**Guerilla warfare** War fought against the ruling power by small, non-professional soldiers, by ambush, bomb attacks, sabotage, etc.

**Latin America** The lands of the western hemisphere which were once part of the Spanish and Portuguese empires, including the whole of South and Central America and Mexico.

**Mandela, Nelson** *See* **African National Congress**

**Marshall Plan** A programme of US aid to European countries, 1948–52, which greatly assisted their economic recovery after the Second World War.

**Microprocessor** The main working unit of a computer, contained in a single silicon 'chip'; developed in the 1970s, it led to much smaller and cheaper computers.

**NATO (North Atlantic Treaty Organization)** An alliance led by the United States and including Canada and most Western European countries, founded in 1949 to defend its members against attack – from the Soviet Union in particular.

**OPEC (Organization of Petroleum Exporting Countries)** An international association of most large oil producers, especially in the Middle East, founded 1961; in the 1970s it raised world oil prices sharply, aided by war in the Middle East.

**Perestroika** The name, meaning 'rebuilding', given to the wide range of liberal reforms introduced in the Soviet Union by Gorbachev in the 1980s.

**Salazar, Antonio** (1889–1970) Portuguese prime minister, 1932–68, who in fact ruled as a dictator, allowing no political parties except his own.

**Satellite** A body that circles a larger one as the Moon – or a spacecraft – circles the Earth; in politics, the Communist states around the Soviet Union and largely controlled by it.

**Taiwan (Formosa)** An island off China ruled by the Kuomintang (Chinese Nationalists) after their defeat by the Communists in 1949; it held the Chinese seat in the UN until 1971.

**Vietnam War** A civil war between Communist North and pro-Western South Vietnam, 1954–75, ending in victory for the North in spite of the large US force fighting for the South.

**Warsaw Pact** A military alliance led by the Soviet Union and including the Communist states of East Europe, founded in 1965 when West Germany became a member of NATO.

**World Bank (International Bank for Reconstruction and Development)** An agency of the UN, linked with the International Monetary Fund, founded 1945 to encourage international financial cooperation; it had a large part in lending money for development to Third World countries.

**Yalta conference** The last meeting (February 1945) of the three chief Second World War leaders, Churchill (Britain), Roosevelt (United States) and Stalin (Soviet Union), held at Yalta in the Crimea (Soviet Union), which made arrangements for Europe after the defeat of Nazi Germany, including the division of Germany into East and West.

# Index

Page references to illustrations are shown in *italic* type.